What Jesus Wants You to Know Today

What Jesus Wants
You to Know Today

About Himself, Christianity, God, the World, and Being Human

GINA LAKE

Endless Satsang Foundation

www.RadicalHappiness.com

Cover art: © agsandrew/DepositPhotos.com

Copyright © 2019 by Gina Lake

ISBN: 978-1097203635

All rights reserved. No part of this book may be used or reproduced by any means, graphic, electronic, or mechanical, including photocopying, recording, taping, or by any information storage retrieval system without the written permission of the publisher except in the case of brief quotations embodied in critical articles and reviews.

To the Christ in everyone.

Contents

Preface	ix
CHAPTER 1 My Life As Jesus and Christianity	1
CHAPTER 2 Your World	37
CHAPTER 3 Being Human	65
CHAPTER 4 Reality	97
Conclusion	129
Afterword	131
About the Author	139
Christ Consciousness Transmissions	141

PREFACE

This book is one of many given to me by Jesus through a process called conscious channeling. When I'm channeling Jesus, I'm essentially taking dictation, as I type the words that I hear Jesus speaking to me mentally into my computer the instant I hear them. These words are as clear to me as if Jesus were sitting next to me, speaking them. I'm able to dialogue with him mentally as well if I want.

Although you may not doubt that Jesus still exists, you may doubt that he can or would communicate with someone in this way. I understand that, and yet he has asked me to share these words with you. And I'm not the only one he communicates with or has communicated with in this way. Over the centuries, he has spoken with countless people. Some were aware that it was Jesus speaking to them and others were not. He is very available to those who are devoted to him and his message of love.

Along with hearing words mentally, I also feel his energy and hear a certain intonation and pace in his speech that is unique to him. Because the words I receive from channeling are experienced quite differently from my own thoughts, it isn't difficult at all for me to tell the difference between the words Jesus is speaking and anything I might think. And unlike my own thoughts, the words of Jesus uplift me.

I hope these words have the same effect on your consciousness. Perhaps that's how you will know the truth of them and trust their origin—by how they affect you. Each of us must decide for ourselves what to believe and what beliefs we will live by. Jesus taught love and peace, and he was a living example of both, which is why he was and is so revered. We know truth when we hear it.

What Jesus has shared in my other books and what he shares in this one, I'm sure, will bring you greater peace and love, and that is the best proof I can think of, of the veracity and value of these words.

Gina Lake
June, 2019

Chapter 1

My Life As Jesus and Christianity

I am the one you have known as Jesus the Christ. I am also you, as I live inside each and every one as the divine consciousness—Christ Consciousness—that everyone is endowed with. I, as Jesus the Christ, am but an external representation of Christ Consciousness, but Christ Consciousness is within you too. I am not the only son of the Father. You are all sons and daughters of this most magnificent intelligence I have called "Father" and many call God.

You are no different than me, in that you have the same potential to be a Christ, to be enlightened, as I was. Indeed, it is everyone's destiny to become enlightened. This is not apparent because you are aware of only this one lifetime that you are living. But if you were familiar with the progression of lifetimes you and everyone else is living, you would see that these lives lead to one thing: enlightenment, which is to say they lead you back home to love, to your own divine nature.

Enlightenment is a state of true seeing, of seeing the truth about who you are and where you came from. This truth is not evident from your ordinary state of consciousness as a human being. You "see through a glass, darkly," and that is the essential difference between you and the Jesus you knew me as and the nonphysical ascended, or enlightened, being that I am now.

I knew the truth and taught the truth when I was alive two thousand years ago, and I am here to offer it to you today, which I can do easily enough with the help of this and other channels. Channeling, or the gift of clairaudience, is a way that people have communicated with those in other dimensions throughout time. Channeling is not new, although it is out of favor with those of a more scientific bent and even with many who are religious, who have been taught that communicating with beings in higher realms only happened to extraordinary people in the Bible and to some saints, not to people today.

It is true that most do not have this ability, but there have always been some who have and who have shared their insights throughout history for the betterment of humanity. Edgar Cayce was one such example.

Regardless of what you think of channeling, it is the way I am able to speak to you today. If you are open and willing to listen, then please read on, for I have much to say to you that relates to my past, your world today, your lives, and your well-being.

I have shared my teachings extensively through this channel, and I will continue to do so here as well. But I also want to share some things about myself, my past, and my perspective on the world that I haven't shared before. These are trying times, indeed, but so much good is also occurring on planet Earth, which I and others like myself are celebrating.

∞

I'd like to begin by explaining who I was and what was and was not true about my life and teachings two thousand years ago. I will also tell you more about my current mission. Accepting this might require suspending some of your beliefs, as some of this information may be unfamiliar or in conflict with what you currently believe. Nevertheless, it is important to me to set the record straight. There is much I'd like to correct and explain so that you understand the truth about my lifetime as Jesus, my teachings, and my current work with humanity.

First of all, let me say that Jesus was but one of my many lifetimes on earth, the most illustrious one from your standpoint, but not from mine. I was a simple man then, standing up for what I believed and teaching the truth as I knew it. I was a spiritual teacher and a healer, but I was no more special than you, no less human and no more divine. I was enlightened, however, and that is what set me apart and what people recognized in me and revered.

In those times, it was uncommon to meet someone who was enlightened, although it is less so today. Many assume that I was a perfect human being or a god, but I was not. I was human, with all the emotions and egoic tendencies of every human being. However, I had learned to master my lower nature, or ego, including my emotions, for the most part, although I still experienced emotions.

I was human *and* I was divine, just as you are. Most people haven't actualized their divine self, or at least to the extent that I and other enlightened or awake beings have. This human life is a journey of discovering and uncovering your divine self and learning to live as that.

What I mean by enlightened is that I didn't have to return to another earthly lifetime after my lifetime as Jesus. I had completed my journey and lessons as a human being, as will each of you at some point. In fact, I had already completed that journey *before* I came into that lifetime. I came then, not for my own evolution, but to fulfill a certain destiny of which you are well aware.

At a certain point during that lifetime, I realized I had a destiny and generally understood what that destiny was, since I was closely in touch with the "Father," or the guidance being given me from higher dimensions. And I was committed to following that guidance regardless of the trials entailed in that.

I knew I would face great difficulties in executing my mission, as humanity was in a very primitive state and, for the most part, deeply ignorant and capable of great cruelty. Despite that, I gladly took on this challenge, for I saw the opportunity to affect many with my sorely-needed message of love. Someone had to come to earth to fulfill this destiny, and I enthusiastically volunteered. I welcomed the opportunity to try to free those I could from their shackles of ignorance.

I also foresaw that, after my death, many of these teachings would be co-opted by egos, distorted, and put in service to a hierarchical religion that would be carried out in my name. Still, the teachings needed to be brought to earth for the relative few who could understand them and pass them on.

My purpose was never to establish a religion, and I understood that people would turn what I said or what they thought I said into a religion. But there was only so much I could do about that or about how people might interpret the teachings after I was gone. That was up to them, and many lessons have resulted from that.

Nevertheless, over the centuries, I've done my best from this dimension to shape these teachings through monks, nuns, priests, ministers, higher authorities in the church, and ordinary people who've been able to connect with me intuitively. I have always been present within the Christian church, behind the scenes, inspiring and leading people to the truth to the extent that I have been able to and to the extent that people have been open to me and to the truth. Despite this, many distortions in my teachings remain.

And I am present in your churches, in the buildings where you worship. My presence in churches is real, and it is felt. That is authentic, even if some of what is taught is inaccurate. Wherever I am called upon, I appear. And whenever you call upon me, I am there. I am real, and I am experienced in people's Hearts. The truth I taught is real, and that is experienced in your Hearts as well.

Many who experience me in these sacred settings tend to trust and believe what the church says because of their very real experience of me. But trusting your experience of me and trusting the dogma of the church are two very different things. This has been very confusing for many: They are having true spiritual experiences within a structure founded on certain untruths. It's not surprising that people were willing to accept certain untruths without questioning them in exchange for the sense of spiritual connection they truly wanted and felt.

I would like all religious and spiritual people to know that they can connect with me anywhere and anytime. No religion or even a church building is needed to experience me and the truth I represent. This truth is the truth of your own divine nature, for that is what you are experiencing when you experience me. All I ask is that you be discriminating about your religious beliefs and accept only those that take you to love. Shortly, I will enumerate the specific distortions or lies within Christianity that you can let go of.

The truth I came to teach is love: "Love your neighbor as yourself" and "Do unto others as you would have them do unto you" — such simple, yet powerful, truths and guidelines that, if applied, could change the world. The truth is simple and it is self-evident, although not easy to practice.

Knowing the truth is the beginning of changing the world. Too many were and still are living according to false beliefs instead of the truth. I came to earth to try to change that, to be a voice in a vast desert of misunderstandings, and I continue to be a voice for truth to the extent that I can from this dimension. I never really left you. I have never ceased being in service to humanity and your beautiful planet.

I came to earth to change people's hearts and minds, but people don't like their beliefs questioned. Those who do this will always be attacked by the ignorant, the narrow-minded, and the power-hungry. Mistaken beliefs come from the ego and support the ego, and egos don't want their monopoly on beliefs disturbed.

Such beliefs uphold the hierarchy and supposed superiority of the few at the top, and I came to earth to topple that, to promote equality, freedom, peace, and happiness for all. If this situation sounds familiar, it's because not much has changed over the centuries. The ego is still in power and creating inequality and *un*happiness for all, even for those at the top. That is the tragedy. The ego's ways ultimately make everyone miserable. No one wins when the ego is in charge.

But how can this change if people don't understand what the ego is and that an ego-driven life is not the only possibility? I came to show people what was possible, not only that they could be happy with little, but that they were, in fact, children of an infinitely wealthy and generous Father, and that a happy and an abundant life is within everyone's reach, not just in a supposed heaven.

Once the truth is understood, inner and outer riches—and contentment—are possible for any and all who are willing to live according to the truth. The truth I speak of is love. Allowing love to guide you in your life is all that is required to live a blessed life, one full of love and other types of abundance: creativity, joy, fulfillment, beauty, and adoration of the one God abiding within everything, giving life to everything.

It is that—the divinity in all—that I came into life to honor and spread the word about. The lowliest and the mightiest in society are equally beloved in the eyes of God, in the eyes of that which is behind all of creation and which lives and breathes through all of creation.

One thing I would like you to understand is that *every* soul, not just me, descends from the Father, from the originator of all life. Everyone is a son or daughter of God. Then, each soul takes on many, many lifetimes—thousands of them—on earth or on some other planet, with the goal of finding its way back to love.

Reincarnation is one of the teachings that was removed from the Bible by the church fathers, who found this idea inconvenient and threatening. The idea of heaven and Hell was much simpler, and it helped keep people in line: "If you do what we tell you and go to church every Sunday, you will go to heaven: if you don't, you will go to Hell." But life is so much more complex than this—and so much more benevolent!

As you progress through your many lifetimes on earth, you eventually learn that you come from love and are made of love, but only after first losing your way by following the ego and experiencing the depths of suffering entailed in that.

When you finally discover the truth that sets you free from the prison of the ego, that is a blessed life, indeed, but that is only the beginning of the journey back home to love. Then, love has to be practiced moment to moment until you *become* that love. When that love has so permeated your being that all karma is balanced and no new karma is being created, you are said to be enlightened, and your soul no longer needs to return to the physical plane.

Once you have graduated from the earthly plane, you continue to exist in higher, nonphysical dimensions, each with its own experiences, lessons, service, and purpose, which the soul continually grows from.

In these higher dimensions, there is no suffering. The suffering you experience on earth is unique to that phase in the soul's evolution. These higher dimensions are the basis for the teachings about heaven. In that sense, heaven is real, as many people who have experienced these higher dimensions as a result of near-death experiences and out of body travels can attest to.

For eons, I have existed in higher dimensions, in the fifth and sixth. I have also tasted the seventh. My life on earth as Jesus was as a savior. That is true, and I will explain what I mean by that shortly. Although returning to the earthly plane from higher dimensions, as I did, may seem like a great sacrifice, I didn't see it that way. Those in higher dimensions exist to serve. It is our joy to do so. It is our reason for being. It is how we give glory to the Father. Throughout human history, higher dimensional beings have regularly reincarnated to serve humanity.

So, I am not special in this. Yes, I came as a savior, but that is happening throughout the universes. Throughout all of creation, saviors are sent to serve those in need. As I have so often said, benevolence is behind creation. Those of us in higher dimensions live for love and live in service to love, and our service is to point those who are lost toward love.

I came to earth to save you from your false beliefs. The only means I had for saving you was to teach you the truth, and that is what I was crucified for, for teaching love. My teachings were felt to be seditious. They upset those in power, who wanted to remain in power.

The authorities believed I was a revolutionary and thought I wanted their power, but they were wrong. I had no use for earthly power, no desire whatsoever for any of the things most people crave and mistakenly believe will make them happy. I knew better. I knew that happiness could never exist where love was not. I came to teach *that*, not grab for power, not even spiritual power.

I did not come to build a church or found a religion, but to correct the distortions within the religion of that day. This is also my intent today, as many of the teachings attributed to me were misunderstood and are distortions of the truth. I'll do my best to correct these misunderstandings here.

∞

The first thing I'd like to clarify is that I did not die for your sins. I came to teach you the truth so that you would stop behaving in ways that harm yourself and others. I came to teach you the way of love, which is also the way of forgiveness.

For that, I didn't need to be crucified. My crucifixion didn't save you or wash away your sins, but it did succeed in making me a martyr, which helped ensure that my teachings lived on. That may be why higher forces allowed crucifixion to be part of my destiny. I was aware of that destiny before I came into a body and then became aware of it again once I was spiritually advanced enough to foresee my fate.

Yes, I came to save people, but from themselves, from their own mistaken beliefs and lack of love by teaching them another way. The events of my life didn't save anyone in that lifetime nor in subsequent ones. No one can actually save you but yourself. No one is freed from the prison of ego by a savior's act, least of all a blood sacrifice. The idea of making a blood sacrifice to win approval or forgiveness from God is pure superstition, a throwback to primitive humankind and their ancient religions. I did not sacrifice my body for you or for any reason.

The savior brings the teachings, and then people must save themselves by applying those teachings in their lives. No one is saved without a commitment and some effort on their part to know the truth and follow it. There is no other way. I and others light the way, but each person must choose to step on the path of love and live it. I repeat: Only you can free yourself from the prison of your ego and its mistaken beliefs.

While I am on the subject of correcting the record, have I made it clear that I am not the one and only son of God nor am I God nor a god, at least not any more than you are? Or I could say this another way: Everyone and everything is God incarnate. God is living within creation.

What this means is that the same consciousness is within everything. This consciousness is sometimes called Christ Consciousness, although there are many other names for it, such as divine light, divine consciousness, Cosmic Consciousness, Essence, Awareness, and the Self.

The same consciousness is looking out of the eyes of every creature who has eyes. Look and see for yourself! The same intelligence is in every living creature's eyes, even those you assume to be far less intelligent than you.

The intelligence I'm speaking of is not the intelligence that can be measured by exams, but the intelligence of life itself. Life is intelligent! Life is intelligent because God is intelligent. This intelligence is of unimaginable brilliance, an intelligence that even I cannot fully fathom.

You are not separate from this intelligence but born from it and, therefore, at one with it. If it were otherwise, you would not exist. Nothing exists apart from this intelligence. There is only one intelligence, and it has manifested all of life.

God is woven into life in such a way that God cannot be separated from it. God is inherent in life in the same way that wetness is inherent in water. Therefore, there is no greater or lesser creation, no hierarchy within creation. That would be like saying your arm is greater than your leg or an apple is greater than an orange (although the ego might claim something like that). Everything that has been created has a place, a function, and a value to the Whole. Everything has an *equal* value in the eyes of God, which created it to be just as it is.

However, although God is behind creation, that doesn't mean that God is behind *everything* that happens within creation, since certain creations, such as yourselves, have been given free will and are capable of being creators in their own right, including creating suffering for themselves and others.

This particular misunderstanding—that God is causing your suffering and perhaps punishing you this way—is one of the more dangerous misunderstandings promoted by religion, for how can you become free of suffering if you don't understand what is causing it? As long as you believe that lie, you will blame God or others or your circumstances for your suffering and not see that you are the one responsible for it. Your mistaken thinking and the negative emotions and actions that flow from your thoughts cause your suffering.

Depending on what you choose to believe and how you choose to respond to life, you create more love in the world or the opposite. When someone chooses to express the opposite of love or cause harm, it is not God that is at fault. God gifted you with the freedom to choose and to create, and you eventually learn from your choices to be better creators, to create happiness instead of suffering. And it is suffering that teaches you this. Suffering points you away from what is anti-life, anti-love.

Your own personal suffering is the so-called punishment you receive for making choices that are not aligned with love. That is the only "punishment," if you will, meted out by God. You are designed to suffer whenever you "miss the mark," which is the meaning of sin. The "mark," the target or goal, is love. You suffer whenever you fall out of alignment with love.

Suffering and joy are part of the guidance system you've been given, the homing device, which when followed, will bring you back home to love. Suffering tells you that you are believing a lie or taking a wrong direction, while joy tells you the opposite. If you don't want to suffer, then stop believing and doing what causes you and others suffering and start believing and doing what brings peace, love, and joy.

The concept of original sin is another serious misunderstanding. There is no original sin. Human beings are not innately bad, but the opposite: Human beings are innately good. *But* they have an ego that causes them to see themselves as separate, lacking, and at odds with life and others, at odds with love. So, they *behave* badly, but they are not bad. They are just mistaken. They misunderstand life.

The ego misperceives life. The ego is the challenge human beings have been given that must be overcome for you to find your way back home to love. The ego is also behind all of your lessons and growth and, therefore, serves your evolution in this dimension.

The early Christians and those before them correctly saw that something within humankind needed reform, or redeeming. But I didn't come to redeem humankind from their sins. From the standpoint of God, redemption is not necessary. Everyone is already forgiven from on high. My teaching on forgiveness is about forgiving yourself and others so that you can move on and not remain stuck in the pain of the past.

And I did not come to redeem humankind from the ego. That would have required annihilating the ego, which is perfectly designed to do what it does. Even if the ego could be annihilated, I would not annihilate what God created. As I said, I came to teach people how to redeem themselves. I came to teach them how to master their own ego and return to love.

In the Bible, the ego is exemplified by Satan. As Satan is said to have tempted me in the desert, the ego, through the voice in the head, tempts people to go against their divine nature, to go against love. The voice in your head tempts you to act selfishly and shortsightedly, to do what is in the ego's self-interest rather than what is best for the Whole to which you are intimately and inextricably connected.

When you go against the Whole and harm others, you also harm yourself. Sin is like hitting yourself, because you also suffer when you cause others to suffer. This is one of humanity's primary lessons, which is why "Do unto others as you would have them do unto you" works so well as a guideline.

There are deep truths in the Bible, including ones that are not understood by most people. But the Bible is also full of untruths and misinterpretations of what I said. Within such a document, it is very difficult to tell truth from fiction. When lies are embedded in deep truths, those truths make the lies seem true.

Most of what the Bible says that I said is true. The most famous quotes attributed to me survived because they are true and were perceived as such throughout history. Truth stands the test of time. But apparently, lies can too when fear is used to keep them in place.

When you hear the truth, something inside you says, "Yes!" That is the spiritual Heart, your divine nature. When your mind is open, you will discover the truth for yourself. But when your mind is closed because it has been programmed with lies, discovering the truth is much more difficult.

One of the most dangerous and damaging lies endorsed by the church is the idea that you cannot trust your own intellect or Heart to know the truth. Teaching children that they cannot trust their God-given inner guidance system and that they must believe whatever they are told by religious authorities, no matter how irrational or false, is anti-God (anti-love), anti-truth, anti-freedom, anti-democracy, and anti-science. I don't think a society built on those values is one you want to live in; and yet, many do.

This wouldn't be such an issue if your elders and those who came before them had known the truth. But look around you. How well is the belief system you've been given serving you and your world? How happy and free are people? Much of the dysfunction in families and societies is due to putting your faith in things that aren't true and not realizing what *is* true: what is true about life and how to live your life and how to be happy and at peace in this world. These are basic things you don't know collectively, although a few do understand the truth.

This is the truth I have come to teach: What is the truth about life? What is the meaning of life? How can you live your best life? How do you relate to others? How do you relate to your emotions? So much understanding is missing in your lives that is essential for living together in peace and harmony as one family of humankind. What does it matter if you know how many miles the earth is from the Sun or who won the Battle of Waterloo if you don't know how to live your life?

What are you teaching your children? For the most part, you teach them what you were taught, but in humanity's case, that is the blind leading the blind. What's most important is not being taught. Instead, religion, which is supposed to be an authority in spiritual matters, is misleading people and too often creating more hatred and conflict in the world, not more love. When a world finds itself this lost, a savior is often sent to bring the truth again to the people.

Fortunately, today there are lots of people bearing this truth, more than ever before in history — so many truth-tellers, so many who know the truth and are providing access to it. This book is but one way truth is being disseminated and but one way that I am disseminating it.

How much more efficient this is than walking across hill and vale preaching sermons to relatively small crowds. Today, thanks to technology, the truth has a real chance of reaching far and wide and taking hold. *And* I am thankful for this "technology" of channeling, without which I wouldn't have a voice in the world today.

You have been sent *many* saviors, including those who are facilitating the dissemination of the truth by way of their technological inventions. They are also serving truth, although not always. As you well know, there's just as much opportunity for technology to spread lies as truth. Nevertheless, those seeking spiritual truth can easily find it today, and those who are promoting and following lies are having *that* lesson.

To return to the misunderstandings and lies propagated by religion, I'll include the concepts of heaven and Hell. Even if God were a punisher, which God isn't, there is no need to punish people or right injustices in a place such as Hell. Any sin you are involved in is instantly "punished," if you will, by the negativity you experience and the contraction you feel in your being when you are involved with it.

Then, if there is further need for lessons around that behavior, karma or life in general will come into play as a teacher and bring you the circumstances needed to balance that behavior. But even karma is not a punisher, but a very wise teacher. The balancing of karma and any necessary learning happens right here on earth, in this lifetime or in another. Some learning also happens in between lifetimes on the astral plane—learning, not punishment.

As for heaven, there certainly are heavenly realms where you will reside after you have become enlightened and have graduated from the earthly plane. But the heaven portrayed by Christianity is too stagnant and overly simplified to match the truth, as your soul is endlessly progressing through various heavenly dimensions and performing various tasks and services as it returns home to the Oneness from which it came.

The teachings about original sin, sin in general, heaven and Hell, God as a punisher, and so many other false ideas were inserted into the Bible as a means for controlling people through fear and guilt and keeping them within the structure of the church. If the church is telling you lies, and you are told that you'll go to Hell if you don't believe those lies, then you are trapped in a detrimental belief system, which will make evolving spiritually much more difficult. Many spend lifetimes adhering to such belief systems until they find the courage to free themselves.

This is not to say that Christianity or religions in general are never helpful. As I said earlier, most people do experience true spirituality and a sense of being connected to something beyond themselves even within rigid religious structures. Religions also provide social support and some useful moral guidelines. And many do minister to the poor and downtrodden.

Unfortunately, even though the church teaches brotherly love, as I did, Christians are often judgmental toward those who don't share their beliefs or who are simply different. And they often don't recognize the hypocritical nature of their judgments. In this way, the ego has corrupted Christianity, and the church doesn't seem to recognize this or try to correct this. Rather, the church tends to fuel a sense of self-righteousness and superiority within their followers that too often leads to conflict with those who don't agree with them.

This is not what I taught. I taught: "Love your neighbor as yourself." Period. No exceptions. I didn't say, "Love your neighbor only if he or she is like you" or "Love your neighbor only if he or she is Christian or heterosexual." I taught that your neighbor is no different than you, that everyone is the same in God's eyes. Everyone *is* God. The same kingdom of heaven is within everyone.

I had no intention of creating a religion, and I was not involved in creating Christianity. And yet, a religion was created in my name. I do not say this in anger, for I am not capable of that emotion. I just want to clarify this to those for whom my name and Christianity seem one and the same.

When I took on this mission, I knew this would happen. I knew my teachings would be misused and misunderstood. That was bound to happen, given the state of consciousness of most of humanity. And so, this had to play out as it did.

But most of you are much more sophisticated than those from ancient times, much more rational and capable of seeing through the lies you've been told. And yet, so many still do not see through them. I hope that what I'm saying here will give some of you the permission you need to think for yourself and decide for yourself what is true. Please remember, I taught love, and any belief that results in unloving behavior cannot be what I taught.

Is it true to be judgmental or is it true to be loving? These are mutually exclusive states of consciousness. If your religious beliefs are causing you to be judgmental and unloving to anyone at all, then you need to question those beliefs. There's no need to ever feel angry or upset or unhappy with or superior to anyone else. That was not my way. These feelings only lead to suffering. Choose love instead. Just choose love. It's so simple, really, much simpler than hatred or disdain.

Judgment and hatred drain your energy. They make *you* unhappy, not only others. That is reason enough to stop judging. "Do unto others as you would have them do unto you." You don't want to be judged, so don't judge others. Let the judging stop. I didn't teach you to judge. God is not judgmental. Only the ego is judgmental.

Some of the lies that became part of Christianity were for the purpose of deifying me, putting me on a pedestal to be worshipped as a god, making me special and superior to you. When I was with you, I did not set myself apart from you in this way, and I would not do this today.

I was not and am not a god, no more than you, as I have said. The church made me into a god by saying that I was born of a virgin, when I wasn't, and also by claiming that I arose from the dead, when I did not. Since no human being has ever accomplished such feats, the logic is that if *I* have, then I must be a god. If you believe those initial lies, that I was born of a virgin and resurrected my body, then it is fairly logical to believe that I am a god or sent from God.

That is how my early followers and the church fathers elevated me to godhood—with lies. But I was mortal, just like you, and I died, just as you will. However, my soul is immortal, just like yours, and continued to exist in another dimension after death, just as yours will. We are both human *and* divine, mortal and immortal.

To claim that I was a god and you are not is one of the more damaging lies in Christianity. It is damaging because it implies that you lack the divine potential that is in everyone, not just me. It's like telling a child that he or she isn't smart enough or good enough when that child is perfectly capable. It's like preventing a bird from being what it has been designed to be by clipping its wings. It is interfering with the potential and right of every human being to be the best he or she can be.

You wouldn't do this to your child, would you? Would you tell your child that he or she isn't good enough? No, out of love, you would tell your child the truth—that he or she is a divine and loving being and that you will support him or her in doing everything possible to manifest that divine potential. You encourage your child to become what he or she can be. You don't call your child sinful and inadequate. The ego does this, not a loving father or mother, not a loving God.

The Christian church shames you, and that is patently unhealthy for individuals and for society. It is dysfunctional. I do not want my name to be part of that. That was not my message. My message was the opposite. The truth is the opposite.

Who or what benefits from calling you bad and me a god? This is an important question. The ego's lies always belie an agenda, a benefit, for it. If you are bad and need redeeming, then someone needs to fill the role of redeeming you. If you believed you didn't need redeeming or that you could go straight to God to be redeemed, then there would be no need for a church or for religious authorities. But the church told you one more lie: You need to go to church to be redeemed because only those whom the church has trained and declared worthy can act as mediators between you and God.

Through these lies, the church made itself indispensable. This is also a convenient way to keep control of the message — only what the church sanctions as true is true. This is another example of how Christianity was corrupted by the ego.

This doesn't make everyone in the church corrupt, but the system they are involved in is corrupt. Religious leaders in the church are dupes as much as anyone else. There is little remedy for this except tearing down the church as you know it, which isn't going to happen unless everyone leaves it, and that hasn't happened yet in nearly two thousand years.

Fortunately, knowledge is power. The truth will set you free from such lies. It will set you free to see yourself as you truly are, as the beautiful, loving, divine being you are and can be even as you live this human life. It will set you free to have a relationship with God yourself, without the need for a mediator, and to discover for yourself that God speaks to you through your Heart. That is where the truth can be found. That is what can be trusted.

The truth can also be found in facts and in science. You were given a rational mind and an intellect, an ability to think and discern, and you are meant to use it. You, after all, are the one who suffers the consequences if you believe lies. It is, therefore, your responsibility to see that you don't believe lies, that you discover for yourself what is true, what the facts are. But for how to live your life, facts aren't sufficient; you will have to rely on the inner guidance system you were given: the Heart.

The church is not so keen on having you follow your Heart because the church benefits from you following its teachings, which are sometimes in conflict with one's Heart. Unfortunately, the church's teachings are inadequate guides for how to live each moment. At best, they provide general moral guidelines, which you have to figure out how to apply to specific circumstances.

The guidance system you were given by God, on the other hand, is a moment-to-moment guidance system: You discover in each moment how to move in life by listening to "the still, small voice within." I will say more about this in another chapter.

For now, I want to return to other concerns I have about what has been done and said in my name. Let's talk about sex, if you don't mind. Another way I was made into a god, and so-called evidence that I was a god, is that I supposedly didn't have sex. This was a myth, of course, since I was as human as anyone and had a wife and children. But it suited the church's purpose to say that I was celibate, which was considered virtuous and befitting a god.

From this lie, it logically followed that if being celibate is god-like and good, then being sexual is bad. The consequence of this lie was that being sexual or even desiring sex became further proof of one's unworthiness as a human being, of one's animal-like, sinful, ungodly nature. And that is the problem with this lie.

As with original sin, this lie leaves you feeling ashamed and divorced from your divine nature. This is one more way that Christianity disavows your true nature and fortifies your lower nature. It tells you that you are your egoic nature, and it denies your divine nature. How ironic! How contrary this is to the true role of religion, which should lead you *toward* God, not take you away from God.

Another unfortunate ramification of believing this lie is that repressing this very natural desire for sex can lead to inappropriate and harmful sexual expressions. Then sex, indeed, becomes a bad thing. Within the church are plenty of examples of what happens when men try to be celibate. Homosexuality, which is a less common but legitimate form of sexuality, is not the problem I'm referring to, but pedophilia: the priest as predator.

Celibacy is not a natural state. It's fine to choose celibacy if you wish, but becoming celibate is not a path to enlightenment. Although some people who are enlightened have lost interest in sex, celibacy is not necessary for enlightenment.

Another lie, which is perhaps the most egregious one, is that Christianity is the one true religion and that people can come to God only through me, Jesus. This lie, like the others, is designed to keep people within the boundaries of the Christian church and prevent them from exploring other religions and beliefs. Like most lies, this one uses fear—the fear of damnation and not getting into heaven—to keep people as followers.

Once you believe this, you become a true-believer and someone who can be recruited to try to talk others into joining the church. After all, you wouldn't want others to be damned. A good Christian would want to save others from that fate. This lie serves the church by keeping people in it and helping to grow it. You now have a really important reason to be a Christian—you will be eternally damned if you aren't!

Is this really how you think life works? Is this really how a loving God would work? This sounds more like the ego, doesn't it? Where is the evidence that Christianity is the one true religion or that I was the only son of God? In the Bible? The Bible is said to provide the evidence for that, but how reliable is the Bible?

So much could be said on the subject of the Bible, but I will say only a few words. Think about the times in which the Bible was written. Imagine, if you can, how different the world and the people living then were from you. Most people had little education and nothing like the kind of knowledge you have access to today. There were no recording devices or communications technologies. Misunderstandings and misinformation abounded, as they do even today. Humankind was in a state of deep ignorance.

What was written about me, which became the Gospels, was written long after my death and pieced together by numerous people, mostly from stories passed on orally. The Gospels contained embellishments, inaccuracies, and fabrications along with the truth. We aren't talking about a carefully chronicled life history recorded by an impartial observer who lived alongside me. The people who wrote the Gospels were ordinary, simple folk, who wrote them well after I was gone, without any special insight, knowledge, or experience of me.

And yet, many of the basic facts and many of the things that I said were preserved correctly or nearly so. But, as I said, the truth mixed with lies is a particularly dangerous combination, even if the lies are relatively few. The most problematic misrepresentations are the purposeful falsifications and the omissions.

A great deal was left out of the Gospels, such as the fact that I studied with spiritual masters in the Far East, that I was married and had children, and that women were my students as well as men. These and many other aspects of my life were left out of the brief accounts of my life in the Gospels, either because such facts were not known or not remembered, or it didn't serve someone's agenda to include them.

What is left out in historical accounts is often as important as what is included. And why some things were left out is important too. What is ascribed to history often has more to do with the historian than the truth. Those who write history always have their own perspectives and agendas, often driven by their egos. It was no different two thousand years ago.

Another reason for some of the distortions in these accounts, particularly in the quotes attributed to me, is that those in the egoic state of consciousness, which is most of humanity, often misunderstand the truths that emanate from higher consciousness. One often has to have had glimpses of the truth to understand the utterances of spiritual masters.

To further complicate matters, what was written down was in a very different language from your own and underwent numerous translations, edits, and modifications over, not only years, but centuries. In those days, it was easy enough to add quotations, modify what I said or did, or omit things I said or did in ways that distorted or falsified the truth, without anyone being aware that had been done. And this *was* done.

One of the best examples of this is the following quote, falsely attributed to me, which as I just said, is one of the most egregious lies in Christianity: "I am the way, the truth, and the life. No one comes to the Father except through me." In this quote, what I said has been both misquoted and misunderstood.

In building a church and making a case for "one true church," this inaccurate quote—this lie—served religious authorities well. Unfortunately, it has led to immeasurable harm in the form of judgment, separation, hatred, and conflict.

That is the result of lies. Lies harm people. They separate people. They cause people to harm others. The truth does not. The truth sets people free and brings them into alignment with peace and love, not the opposite.

∞

Many of you are probably wondering about what my life as Jesus was like. So, I will say a little about that. I've already covered some of the inaccuracies about my life story: I was not the son of God, I was not a god, I was not born of a virgin, I did not raise my body from the dead, I was not celibate but married with children, and I had no intention or desire to found a church in my name.

On a more minor note, I was dark, with curly dark brown hair and dark brown eyes, as most people in this area of the world were. I was not as handsome as I am often depicted. My features were not as symmetrical. However, I have often appeared to people in a guise more similar to what people expect me to look like so as to meet their expectations.

Please know that any depiction you have of me can be used to connect with me, so how I actually looked is not important at all. That was just a temporary body that served me well in that lifetime.

I was born of a deeply spiritual mother and father who were informed through a vision before I was born that they would be given a special child, one who would be a spiritual leader. Knowing this, they allowed me a lot of latitude when I was growing up to express myself and develop my talents. My parents trusted me, supported me, and gave me the freedom I needed.

At a very young age, I had access to special knowledge. I could mentally dialogue with higher dimensional beings, who guided me and helped me discriminate fact from fiction within the Scriptures of that time and even regarding mundane matters. I learned things from these higher dimensional beings that were not generally known and not written anywhere. As a result, I gained a reputation for being a very bright and insightful boy.

I also received early training from the secretive community known as the Essenes, which was not far from where my family lived. This community's purpose was to gather and store arcane knowledge from near and far. I benefited greatly from their metaphysical and spiritual knowledge, which few people had access to.

Even when I was quite young, people were attracted to me and interested in hearing what I had to say. This gave me a taste of what it would be like to be a teacher. I wanted more than anything to learn more and become a teacher, although I wasn't sure what that would look like until much later.

I had an inquisitive and restless nature. I didn't want to live a conventional life. I wanted to be free to travel and explore various philosophies. But more than anything else, I wanted to right the injustices and expose the hypocrisy that was so apparent to me in the religious leaders of my day.

It was obvious to me that most of the religious leaders were not holy people who understood the truth. They were just playing a role and enjoying holding a superior position in society. Meanwhile, people were suffering at their hands as a result of their harsh judgments and rigid rules. People were also suffering at the hands of the Romans, who were oppressing people for their own reasons. I wasn't sure what I could do about this, but I was sure that I wanted to try to do something.

But first, I needed to develop further. I yearned for even more knowledge than my community could provide. As a young man, I yearned to travel. I had heard of great spiritual masters who lived in faraway places such as India, and I longed to meet them and study with them. This was a dream of mine.

The trouble was, this meant leaving my family and friends for quite some time and, in particular, a woman I was deeply in love with, whom you know as Mary Magdalene. Mary was deeply spiritual as well and understood me. We knew we were meant to be together, and we pledged ourselves to each other. But I was not ready to marry yet, not until I had explored further on my own.

I did get my chance to travel to the Far East, where I wandered from place to place. I would hear about a master and then go to wherever he was. One of the most important things I discovered was that the teachings of these masters were similar to what I had been receiving within myself. This helped me trust the path I'd been on and the destiny I sensed for myself.

I had been told that I had a special destiny, but I had my doubts, naturally. I learned that these spiritual masters were similarly guided and that those with such a destiny often knew that at a young age. Meeting these masters confirmed to me my path in life so that I could continue on with greater confidence.

I felt at home with these wise men, and they had shown me what was possible—what it was to be a spiritual master. Nevertheless, I felt compelled to return home. I was needed there more than I was needed in India. In my land, there was great suffering due to ignorance and oppression, and I was sure that I was meant to try to relieve that in some way. So, I left.

Once I returned, I knew it was time to marry and create a home with Mary. So, my energy went into that for a time, and we started a family. But always, my focus and our focus was on what was closest to both of our hearts: expanding our spiritual awareness and understanding. We meditated together, and I regularly shared the insights I received with her.

I continued to grow spiritually during this time even though my activities were quite mundane. I worked as both a carpenter and a fisherman, which supported us. But life has a way of moving along, and one day, while being baptized by my cousin, John the Baptist, I was "struck by lightning," so to speak, or the spiritual energy known as Kundalini. This changed everything. I didn't realize it at the time, but what I was experiencing was enlightenment.

This spiritual transformation required many weeks of solitude and contemplation to integrate. This period of solitude was the forty days and forty nights in the desert spoken of in the Gospels, although it was not actually spent in a desert environment and it was not exactly forty days and nights. During this time, I didn't experience temptation as much as a clear seeing of the human ego, which as a result, lost any remaining power it had.

After this, I was never the same. I was no longer human in the same way. I saw things differently, including literally, as I was able to see the energy and light in people and read them like never before. This was one of the gifts that opened with enlightenment, along with the healing abilities documented in the Gospels. People were healed in my presence: physically, emotionally, and spiritually, for these are related. Miracles did happen.

Enlightenment was the beginning of my public life as a teacher and healer, which is described in the Gospels fairly accurately, as are the events leading up to the crucifixion and the crucifixion itself. So, I won't say much more about this most significant period of my life, which most of you are already familiar with. I will just say that well before the crucifixion, I knew that I would be crucified for the threat I posed to both the political and religious authorities of my time, and I accepted this fate.

I'd also like you to know that the crucifixion was not as painful as it seemed. For much of the time on the cross, my consciousness had separated from my body before leaving it permanently, which is not unusual in the midst of trauma. Becoming unconscious in such circumstances is a self-protective mechanism, which animals experience as well.

I was sorrowful for my family, of course, but those in power could not allow me to have a voice, and I understood that. I also knew that my teachings would live on in some form. My teachings are fairly well presented in the Bible in the quotes that have survived me, limited as they are, except in a few important instances, as already noted.

After the crucifixion, I did appear occasionally in a light-body to others. This body seemed real to them, so there was reason for some to believe that I had resurrected my body, even though that was not the case. I am by no means the only person who has died and reappeared to others in a seemingly real body, which I was able to manifest through intention. This is an ability that spiritual masters have if they choose to use it.

Since my death, I have remained devoted to earth and the evolution of humanity. I am connected and available to anyone who is devoted to me and my message of love. It is always possible for you to reach me if you have that intention. So, please feel free to call upon me.

∞

Now, I would like to explain who or what I am now and what my role is in relation to earth. In doing this, you will also get a glimpse of your own future beyond the earth plane.

Like all souls who have graduated from the physical dimension, which includes earth and all other physical worlds, I have continued to evolve in higher, nonphysical dimensions. This evolution, and yours, is always for the good of the Whole. Creation is designed to serve creation. All of creation, on the physical plane and beyond, is intertwined and interconnected. Every action that is taken reverberates throughout creation. What you do matters, and what we do matters.

Those at the higher levels of evolution serve those at the lower levels. We, at higher levels, are endowed with skills to serve you, both humanity as a whole and individuals. We serve those on the physical plane in various ways, mostly by providing guidance intuitively and shaping events to the extent that that is necessary and possible.

Guardian angels are not a myth, but a reality, although those performing this function are not usually angels but spirit guides and other ascended beings who have had earthly lifetimes. Angels are not in this category. Others beyond us are guiding us in a similar way.

The creative intelligence, or God, has a plan for those on the physical plane, and we are given knowledge of that plan once it is formed. This plan is not as set as you might think. The creative intelligence is playing it by ear, and the plan unfolds moment to moment, organically, as free-will choices are made by those within creation and as directions come into focus. The creative intelligence has certain goals or intentions, but exactly how those intentions are achieved depends on the choices made within creation.

We have some ability to influence these free-will choices, and when that is necessary, we help shape the direction in which things are going to ensure that the creative intelligence's intentions are met in some way. This is my work. But more specifically, my work entails the evolution of humanity and of certain individuals critical to that. I don't guide individuals in their personal lives, as spirit guides do, but I often have a hand in guiding anyone who might affect the larger picture on earth.

For instance, I'm not a personal guide for this channel except to the extent that it affects our work together. I'm not a personal guide for anyone. I don't give specific advice to people about their lives through any of my channels, but only more general teachings and advice. I am a world teacher, not a spirit guide.

This is also generally true of the ascended masters I work with. We work, often together, to influence what is happening on earth to the extent that we are allowed to and able to. What we are allowed to do and what we can do is limited by certain rules we must follow and by the simple fact that we aren't always able to influence people's choices.

Free will is free. However, people are often quite easily influenced intuitively or by other people's suggestions or by changing circumstances. Those are the tools we have at our disposal to shape people's choices in directions that would be best for the Whole.

Although many choices that people make don't matter, some are crucial, and those are the ones we are likely to try to shape, whether it is a spirit guide doing this or an ascended master. Usually, the more important a choice is, the more beings, including ascended masters, get involved in trying to shape that choice.

The most dramatic interventions are ones where circumstances are designed to change someone's direction. I'm sure you have all experienced this, where something shocking and probably unwelcome happened that caused you to shift your focus or change directions. Such events are likely to have been specifically designed to serve a purpose in your life.

I said that I am a world teacher. What I mean by this is that I work through channels such as this one to bring through information and teachings that will be useful to humanity. I also work with those who are important to humanity's plan intuitively and while they are sleeping, when receptivity is often the greatest.

I have been working with humanity in these ways ever since I departed the body of Jesus and well before that as well. Long before that lifetime as Jesus, I had graduated from the earthly plane. So, I came into that lifetime already an ascended master.

This is one reason I had such easy access to powers you consider miraculous. What happened to me when I became enlightened and why it was so dramatic and complete is that I regained the enlightenment that I had already attained in a former lifetime.

You might be surprised to learn that this is the situation with many today, as many already enlightened beings have descended to earth during these critical times to "save" it, as I did. Most of them do not display the miraculous powers I did, usually because this would be counterproductive in your world. In my lifetime, these miracles helped convince people that what I was teaching was true. But, for the most part, such miracles tend to be more disruptive than helpful. I will say more about those who have more recently come to serve humanity in the next chapter.

In addition to being a world teacher, I and other ascended masters are also healers, as I was in my lifetime as Jesus. We transmit healing energy to anyone who asks for it and is open to receiving it, particularly to those who are healers, such as energy healers and spiritual teachers. Many of today's alternative healers and spiritual teachers are higher dimensional beings who came to earth to be of service, and we work through them to heal and raise the level of consciousness on earth.

We also transmit healing energy to the planet and other entities that can benefit from it, such as certain species of animals that are under duress. We can also affect some of the systems that maintain earth's homeostasis, or balance.

As with influencing someone intuitively, we are only allowed to influence someone's healing to the extent that they allow that and to the extent that it doesn't interfere with their lessons and soul's plan. Because people have free will, they are free to open or close to those in higher dimensions, and we are bound to honor that choice.

Most of those who are closed to us are not aware that they are closed and not consciously choosing that, but we still must honor that and, therefore, don't become involved. People are either immersed in their egoic thoughts or not, and that is essentially what determines whether someone is open to us or not. When someone is immersed in their egoic thoughts, it could be said that they are choosing those thoughts, since they aren't seeking anything beyond that. And until they do, we can affect them only so much.

Everyone, no matter what their state of consciousness, receives guidance and healing from other dimensions to some extent. But by making a more explicit intention to receive guidance and healing, you will receive even more. This is why I so often encourage people to pray and ask for what they want and need. That way, we have permission to intercede more fully.

Such an intention or prayer is often made when people find themselves suffering deeply. Then, they often call out for help, and we answer. We allow people to have whatever experience they are having until they state that they are ready to have a different experience. Then, we can transmit healing energy to them and help them learn whatever they need to learn from that experience so that they can move on.

I said before that I'm not a personal guide, but I *am* a personal healer. If you call upon me for healing, then you will receive that. This healing may be spiritual, emotional, or physical. It may also take other forms, such as insights, opportunities, or gifts that ease your way. The reason that I and other ascended masters are so available to anyone for healing is that healing you is a means of raising your vibration, your state of consciousness, and that is one of our specific jobs at this time. We are tasked with raising humanity's consciousness, and that happens one person at a time.

We also transmit energy to groups of people: "Wherever two or more are gathered together, there I am." When you gather with others with an intention to evolve and heal and you call upon me or other ascended masters, we arrive bearing the gifts you need to accelerate your spiritual evolution.

A large part of this acceleration entails helping you heal your psychological wounds. If you ask us for healing, we will help bring certain emotional complexes to the surface and then provide you with the intuitions, insights, and healing energy you need to heal them. We facilitate your own natural course of evolution. With our help, this evolution can happen more quickly and more smoothly.

Your intention is critical in this healing process. Your intention notifies us of what you are ready and willing to acknowledge within yourself and heal. There's a time for everything, as they say, and your intention to heal something tells us you have enough awareness and will to cooperate with your own healing. Without that, there would be no point in sending you assistance.

Healing is a cooperative venture between us. You say, "Yes, I'm ready and willing to heal x," and we help you with that. But you will also have to cooperate with the ways we are helping you heal. For instance, we may send you a healer to help you or a book to help you or an insight to ponder. During the healing process, we communicate with you in these various ways: through other people, books, and intuitions.

So, you see, this healing process isn't passive. There is work you are expected to do. And the proof that you truly are ready to heal something is that you are willing to take steps to heal or open to insights or do some inner investigation on your own.

And now, perhaps enough has been said to set the stage for me to tell you some of my perceptions about your world, its problems, and what can be done about them.

Chapter 2

Your World

Most of you reading this probably have a similar view of the situation in the world. You are most likely concerned about what you see going on, on many levels: the changing climate, environmental pollution and degradation, overpopulation, the unequal distribution of wealth and resources, terrorism and war, and racial prejudice and inequality. These are but a few of humanity's most pressing issues.

I don't claim to be able to solve these problems for you, but there are solutions, since your problems essentially stem from humanity's state of consciousness. This may sound simplistic, and yet it is true. We have witnessed worlds like your own go through similar types of transformations, some that have succeeded and some that have not. Success in solving your problems comes down to choosing love over the self-interest of individuals and nation states. This is why raising people's state of consciousness is the answer to transforming your world. Love is the answer.

Love will make it possible for you to come together as one world, and that is what needs to happen and what is trying to be born from all this pain and suffering. There is a natural evolution that worlds undergo, and becoming a global society is the next step in humanity's evolution.

For some worlds, this need for unity is clear and accepted, while for others, unifying in this way is seen as the problem rather than the solution. They don't want this to happen for many reasons, but most of those are based on fear, prejudice, or self-interest.

In transitioning to a global society, people will have to make changes and adapt. Some will lose their jobs, while others will gain jobs. Just as your personal identity must undergo changes at times, so must your national identity. To become one world, you must become more inclusive and more tolerant, and you must recognize that peace is impossible without equality, without a more equal distribution of goods and without you becoming "your brother's keeper."

In short, you must open your hearts to others, or you may all perish. You are in the same boat, and that boat is sinking. "Every man for himself" is not going to save you. You must pull together before it is too late. How many movies have you seen that have depicted this, where the characters were in dire straits, but by working together, they saved themselves?

Yes, many of your movies are about a superhero saving humanity, and many of you are hoping for that. There have been many "superheroes" among you who have swooped in and saved you from one thing or another. But one superhero or a group of ETs is not going to save humanity except possibly to remove some surviving humans from earth after you have destroyed it. But that's hardly the happy ending most are looking for.

When you are in trouble, you have to rely on your inner resources. That's what a superhero does and that's what each of you will have to do. The answers to what you need lie within you, and you must pool your resources to come up with the best solutions. This is already happening across the globe, and so much more is possible given your connectedness with each other. If two heads are better than one, then imagine what seven billion can do, especially when they are under pressure to find solutions. So, there certainly is hope for your world.

One of the problems is that you aren't in agreement about what your problems are. Climate change is an example. Before you can find a solution, you have to agree that something is a problem. And in other cases, such as overpopulation, you are aware of the problem and some relatively simple solutions, such as making contraception available to everyone who needs it, but the will is not there to implement those solutions.

If you don't willingly reduce your population, people will continue to suffer in various ways at the effect of that. Your planet is already at full occupancy. Reducing the population would ameliorate every other problem in your world. And yet, so few seem to acknowledge this as the major problem that it is or do anything about it. Bringing fewer people into the world is a much simpler solution to overpopulation for everyone than people dying of hunger, disease, and war.

Once you have identified your problems, you need the capital, from government or private parties, to finance those who can best find solutions. Entrepreneurs in Silicon Valley and elsewhere have already achieved tremendous feats and are on the verge of great discoveries that will transform your world. What lags behind and often delays your progress is politics— the inability to get governments to back what is beneficial for society and for your future.

New forms of energy are an example. Your governments are clinging to current ways of providing energy when it is apparent that you will need alternatives to fossil fuels. Until governments operate on the basis of what is best for society and for your future rather than at the behest of the powers that be and special interest groups, governments will fail the public and fail the future.

Politics has been corrupted by the few with power, who use their power to bend the government to their will. Rather than serving the people, governments too often serve the wealthy few, resulting in the status quo being upheld when what is most needed is vision and innovation.

Those in power who are invested in outdated energy sources won't hand over that power easily. How do you move them out of power or at least get an even playing field so that new technologies and energy sources can take hold? This is the age-old problem of the old needing to make way for the new, which is particularly challenging today because those in control of the old ways are especially powerful politically.

This problem may seem insurmountable, but it isn't. There are just a few changes that will make a big difference. People will vote for what is most important to them if they have a vote, and that is what democracy is about—rule by the majority. People will vote for clean energy, a clean environment, good schools, and affordable healthcare. Democracy gives power to the people to make choices that benefit the majority rather than a small group of individuals. If what's going on in government is not benefitting the majority and not benefiting society—and it isn't—then that needs to be fixed.

In the United States, simply eliminating the electoral college and reforming gerrymandering would go a long way toward putting the power back into the hands of the majority. These systems have meant that many of you are not being fairly represented. Your votes have not counted. In the case of the electoral college, for instance, if your vote isn't like the majority in your state, your vote doesn't count.

Then, money must be removed from the election process. This can be accomplished easily enough by the government (through a small tax) giving all candidates the same amount of money and airtime for their campaigns. If taxpayers are paying for elections, then elections can't be corrupted by a few wealthy donors buying candidates and influence.

This simple change would be truly democratic. If money is determining who runs and who wins, which it does to some extent, that is the definition of corruption. From the start, your election process is corrupt. And from there, money continues to influence what laws get passed and where your taxes go. This, too, has to change. Money must be removed from politics. This is obvious, and yet nothing is done about it.

The cost of campaigns to the public could be kept to a minimum by reducing the length of time that candidates campaign and by giving voters straightforward information about the candidates' positions—just the facts without the spin and attacks. In this day and age, there is no reason for people to campaign like they did before there was such widespread media accessibility. These are just a few obvious changes that would make your system fairer for all.

And on this subject, does the majority really want to spend a disproportionate amount on military defense? Every dollar spent on defense is a dollar not spent on strengthening education, healthcare, infrastructure, and other areas of keen interest and obvious benefit to most people. The military is an area that needs deep reexamination and reorientation. A great deal of money is being spent maintaining a military and military machinery, much of which is outdated, given the cyber age. Your fear and belief in war is very, very costly to society.

I also want to say something about the importance of honesty in politics. The more you, the public, let your politicians get away with lying and the more you vote for those who lie, the more likely your system will fail. Honesty is the cornerstone of a healthy democracy. The public must demand honesty of all public officials and politicians or your political system will devolve into whomever can most effectively lie wins.

You are being challenged now to find a way to keep lying in check, while continuing to honor the First Amendment. But if free speech means giving free rein to politicians to manipulate the public with lies, you won't have much of a democracy left. This is one of the most important issues you have to deal with now, the issue of determining fact from fiction and calling false information out in a way that prevents those who would manipulate your system with lies from gaining power.

Politicians should be held to a higher standard regarding their speech. It should not be acceptable for them to lie, meaning willingly and knowingly mislead the public. If they do this while in office, this is cause enough for impeachment, particularly if those lies are designed to manipulate people's perceptions of reality, veil the truth, create division, and incite violence.

Is this not how dictators manage to gain and hold power? Is this not the difference between authoritarian regimes and democracies? The First Amendment is, in part, meant to protect the public from those who might oppress them through manipulation and lies. It gives people the freedom to protest and speak out against any government injustices and abuses of power. Free speech was not intended to be a tool for enabling political oppressors. It is not meant to include the freedom for politicians to lie to the people. If you aren't careful, you could lose your freedoms altogether by not checking the speech of your politicians and not requiring truthfulness.

The responsibility for determining what is true and untrue usually falls to journalists. But when good journalists are no longer trusted or when journalists are no longer truth-tellers, then who determines what is true and not true? Undermining the credibility of good journalists is the first step in the downfall of a democracy, the first step toward authoritarianism. Like politicians, journalists must be held to a high standard, and those who don't follow such a standard shouldn't be considered journalists.

This hasn't been a significant problem until the rise of so many unreputable internet news sites. Because of generally good journalism practices over the years, the public had largely come to trust the news they were given. Now, you know better, and that is good. There are a number of bad players out there, including those attempting to undermine your democracy, who think nothing of using certain news sites to spread lies for their own nefarious purposes.

One reason people are falling prey to false news is that they aren't educated sufficiently. People whose knowledge base is inadequate are easily fooled by lies. Lies can be very convincing when mixed with a few facts. For democracy to work, the public must have access to good education and good information and be motivated to understand their world and their government.

Poverty is one of the main reasons people are not educated sufficiently. In the United States, poverty means inadequate schools and education. The problem with your educational system is that you pay for schools with property taxes, which early on, stacks the deck against those who are not well off.

Poverty and the resulting lack of equal opportunity for education and other benefits that those from wealthier families take for granted too often produce angry and unhappy youth, who are vulnerable to negative influences. Because of poor schools, children from poor families have much more difficulty becoming productive members of society than those who grow up with more advantages. Give all children good schools, and most children can overcome the disadvantages of growing up in poverty.

Unequal education results in an uneven playing field, which aggravates class distinctions and increases the gap between levels of society. When this gap becomes large enough, the result is resentment, anger, and a sense of victimization in those who perceive themselves to be marginalized with no chance of achieving "the American Dream."

This situation is amplified by television and other media, which depict the enormous amounts of wealth, power, and privilege that some have. This disparity in wealth is becoming an increasing problem, as it creates resentment, discontentment, and unhappiness even in those who are living comfortable and relatively affluent lives.

When most of the wealth in your country and in the world is in the hands of a few people, that's not only bad for those suffering economically and bad for society, but also bad for those with extreme wealth. It gives a few people too much power, and power does corrupt most people. At the very least, too much money leads to endless seeking after that which can never satisfy or lead to happiness.

If those with the most wealth were enlightened, this situation might not be such a problem. But often those who accumulate vast wealth are driven by their ego's greed and desire for power, and they shouldn't be in power and wouldn't be if it weren't for their ill-gotten gains. The ego knows how to get money and power and will often stop at nothing to get it, but the ego doesn't know how to use it well.

There are certainly billionaires who got there by providing something of real value to society, and society can be grateful to them and is glad to reward them. But, generally, so much money in the hands of so few is not a healthy situation for anyone.

∞

So much is being learned by everyone through these difficult times! The wealthy are learning that money can't buy happiness and that unless that wealth is shared, making money your god is an empty life indeed. The poor are learning quite different lessons. Theirs usually relate to developing the talents they need to lift themselves out of poverty and, perhaps more importantly, developing their inner strengths, such as courage, compassion, and perseverance.

To succeed, those economically challenged must overcome any tendencies to feel victimized, angry, and resentful, which is no small task, especially if one's environment is filled with fear and negative emotions. If they can develop in these ways, then their environment can be said to have served them by making them stronger. Poverty is just one of many challenges the soul takes on to make you stronger, more compassionate, and possibly more passionate about helping others in a similar situation.

Many who are poor turn to spirituality, religion, or family for their happiness and sense of fulfillment, and that is a good choice, a positive choice. Such circumstances are often chosen by souls whose life purpose relates to emotional or spiritual growth.

The circumstances you were born into were an important and a meaningful choice on the part of your soul. Your family and early childhood situation were chosen to shape you in some way, to bring you the lessons you need and steer you toward developing certain talents central to your life purpose. Those circumstances were designed by your soul to provide you with certain experiences and challenges to help you grow in the ways you need to grow. They were not a mistake.

How this choice works out for the soul depends on that person's choices and on the free-will choices of others in that environment, which the soul has little control over. The soul is never certain if the chosen circumstances will actually serve the person's growth, as hoped, or not. In some instances, the chosen circumstances hinder growth and the fulfillment of the life purpose. When that happens, spirit guides and other light beings intervene to attempt to shift that situation.

It is very important that you don't use the idea that someone's soul might have chosen a particular challenge as an excuse to not help that person. You are God's hands. You are God's helpers. You are the main way that God can affect situations in the world because, without a body, light beings can only do so much. You are meant to be the instruments of God, and light beings provide your instructions intuitively.

Everyone is being communicated to by spirit guides and other light beings through their intuition. But since not everyone has easy access to their intuition and not everyone listens to it, God often relies on those of you who have better access to your intuition to help others—to give them the messages, information, or assistance they need. God moves you intuitively to give others a helping hand.

You are your brother's keepers. By this, I don't mean you should give people everything they need or ask of you. And I don't mean that you must be the one to help everyone. Sometimes, that help is meant to come from someone else, in which case, you won't be inspired to help. Your intuition will tell you whether to give and when and what to give.

What I mean is that you are instruments of the Whole for taking care of the Whole. All of humanity is like one body. If you are tuned in intuitively, you will know what is being asked of you in terms of service to others. Learning to serve in this way is one of your lessons as a human being. Everyone must learn to tap into their inner guidance and allow themselves to be run by that.

Learning to operate this way is part of your spiritual unfoldment and essential to enlightenment. Enlightenment means knowing yourself as everyone and everything, and when that is the case, you naturally take care of what needs taking care of. You answer the call to service in your corner of the universe. Anyone who says that he or she is enlightened and is not sensitive to the needs of others and serving them in some way is probably not fully enlightened.

It seems important to say something here about karma. Being born into poverty or with any other type of challenge is not a sign of bad karma. It does not mean you are being punished for something you did in the past. Life does not punish; it teaches. This is so important to see.

Such misunderstandings about karma result in people being callous and unkind, which is how the ego responds when presented with someone in need. The ego makes up excuses for not helping, for not feeling or caring, so that it can go on its merry way taking care of Number 1.

What the ego doesn't appreciate is that everyone is part of the Whole and everything affects the Whole. So, when you take care of others, you are taking care of yourself; when you neglect others, you neglect yourself. "Whatsoever you do to the least of my brethren, you do to me."

What you do in life does matter. It matters to your soul, and it matters to the Whole. What you put out creates your experience of life: When you put out kindness, that comes back to you. When you put out hatred, that comes back to you. This is karma. This is how life teaches you how to behave. If you want to be happy, be kind. If you want to be unhappy, be unkind.

It's really that simple — and obvious. It is obvious enough which behaviors bring happiness and good results and which ones don't. What isn't obvious is how to change your automatic reactions to life: how to stop being your ego and start behaving as your divine self. Very few actually teach this, but teaching this is part of my mission.

This can be taught, but the hard part is practicing the teaching, applying it moment to moment. That takes not only an understanding of how to move out of the ego and into the divine self, how to shift your consciousness, but also the will to do this when you find yourself caught in ego. That is the hard part. But with practice, that choice becomes easier and eventually becomes how you *are* in life. With enough diligence and practice, you will become the divine human being you are meant to be, of which I was but one example.

Part of the problem in making this shift in consciousness is that models for how to be in the world in this new way are few, including in the media. Yes, there are always moments in movies and TV when good prevails and you applaud the good in people, but mostly what you see in movies and TV are people struggling with their demons, and sometimes actual demons. You are very familiar with how people who are driven by their egos behave, but you have far fewer examples of how those who are aligned with their divine self behave, those in a higher state of consciousness.

Furthermore, your ideas about what that would look like are distorted. You think, "I can never be a saint, and I don't know any saints." But progress on the spiritual path doesn't look like your idea of sainthood. Saints don't even look like your idea of sainthood. So, that's one thing that needs to be clarified: You need a clear understanding of what spiritual progress looks and feels like.

Here is how it looks: It looks like being in the flow; being at ease with life, with others, and with yourself; being grateful and content with the way things are; being kind and accepting of others; being fulfilled by doing what you are moved to do; finding joy in little things and in just being alive; and being your best self. This is sainthood, this is enlightenment, and this is everyone's destiny.

You already know how it feels to be a saint or enlightened, because in your best moments you *are* that. Your best self may be covered over much of the time, but it has always been there, and it peeks out every so often, or perhaps quite often for some of you. Many today, in fact, are living as that much of the time. There is a movement afoot, to be sure. People are waking up and learning to live as their best self, and this is what I am here to help you with.

∞

It is no mistake that many are waking up today to their divine self in unprecedented numbers. As I said, something is afoot, and that something is very mysterious and may be difficult for some to believe. Whether you believe this or not, I'd like to ask you to set aside your doubts for a moment, while I explain what I mean more fully.

At critical points in the history of every world, saviors are sent to supply the knowledge, wisdom, and truth needed by that world to help it in its evolution. The worlds I am speaking about are ones with some kind of sentient humanoid lifeform.

It may not come as a surprise to many of you that you are not alone in the universe. Many imagine that there are others like yourselves out there somewhere. Well, there aren't—not humanoids exactly like you, but many, many other types of humanoids.

You, on earth, are unique. As you may have noticed, God doesn't tend to duplicate what has already been created, but relishes creating new and unique lifeforms. Your uniqueness makes humanity very precious to those watching over you, who have carefully nurtured and guided humanity for millennia.

It took humanity a very long time to arrive at the point where you could destroy your entire civilization. Many worlds get to this point, and some make it and some don't. We aren't quite sure what will happen to humanity, to be honest. But we are doing our best to help humanity to not only survive but thrive.

As I said, many worlds at such junctures have required a savior or saviors to intervene to help things along. In your case, many saviors have been sent from higher dimensions to yours in the form of seemingly ordinary human beings who are not actually so ordinary. I will call these saviors Star People, as many before me have.

Star People are ascended beings who reincarnated on earth because they were needed and because they volunteered, as I did two thousand years ago. They are born in the same way as any other human being or they "walk in" to a body as another soul leaves it. Today, Star People are involved in every field and human endeavor, working as transformers and bringing in new ideas.

Star People are able to physically be of help to a world by being in the world, while I and other light beings can only help from afar. What we do from higher dimensions is inspire scientists and others to create things that will improve lives. Benjamin Franklin and Nikola Tesla are examples of people who regularly received guidance from us. We also guide people, such as the founding fathers in the United States, in developing political systems and laws that will make societies freer and stronger. And we inspire artists and musicians to create works that bring people into a higher state of consciousness. We work through everyone who is open to us to create a better world. Our means of influencing people is primarily through their intuition and through dreams and visitations.

These types of activities are always being carried out between higher dimensions and the physical dimension. But when a world needs more help than this or when people become so lost that they aren't receiving sufficient help through the usual means, a savior or saviors are often sent.

Although Star People look like any other human being, they often stand out in various ways. Most have a particular talent or genius or a special connection to the higher dimensions that allows them to receive information easily. They act as telephones or conduits to higher dimensions, where they receive large quantities of information: in dreams, in visions, through channeling, or through what feels like downloads of information. Some Star People are aware of their mission, while many are not.

Look around you, and it's not difficult to see that this is going on. Most of your giant leaps in technology have been instigated by those with a connection to special information that others don't have access to.

Star People are enlightened beings in disguise. Some of them have regained their enlightenment partially or fully and appear awake or enlightened, while others have not and do not appear that way. Sometimes, enlightenment would just get in the way of accomplishing what they came here to do. Most Star People will regain their enlightenment to the degree that that would facilitate their work.

You might imagine that being fully enlightened would always be beneficial, but enlightenment is not always the most practical or functional state. Because my mission included being a spiritual teacher, for me, full enlightenment served. But if a scientist became fully enlightened, for example, he or she might discontinue those pursuits or be considered so odd that his or her work might not be supported by the scientific community.

A certain amount of ego and drive is often necessary to accomplish things in the world, and someone who is fully enlightened is more likely to drop out of the busy-ness of the world than stay in it. So, if your life purpose requires some ego and involvement in the world, then regaining full enlightenment probably wouldn't serve.

Star People are often unique, original, and march to their own drummer. They tend to be unconventional, non-traditional, and not inclined to follow the crowd or even the mores of society. They are the ones most likely to point out what isn't working and to come up with original solutions and to point out that "the emperor has no clothes." Star People think outside the box and see things from a higher perspective.

Their lack of conventionality can be disconcerting to family members and more conventional types, who don't understand the Star Person and may find him or her unreliable or even threatening. Consequently, Star People often leave their families behind and make their way alone or find others who are more like them whom they can relate to.

Star People also tend to be humanitarian, egalitarian, and pantheistic or spiritual rather than religious, as they have a natural and easy connection with the intelligence behind life. They often have a sense of belonging elsewhere than on earth and yearn for their lost heavenly home. On some level, they remember where they came from and know they will return.

Most Star People have a strong sense of mission or destiny and are self-directed and intensely driven from within. This can cause them to appear arrogant and headstrong at times. They are determined at all costs to pursue what they feel they need to do to unfold their destiny.

There are well over a million Star People on earth today—more than ever before in history—which gives you an idea of the importance of the times in which you are living. You *do* have the power to destroy yourselves and the ecological balance on earth to the degree that it could no longer sustain human life. This is of deep concern to those of us guiding humanity and your planet. This would be a grave loss to the Whole.

You see yourselves as separate and apart, alone in the universe. But you are far from alone. There are countless humanoid species in the universe. But that aside, you are also connected to many, many others on other dimensions. You *are* us—who we were; and we are you—who you will be. We are the same.

Just as you want your children to succeed in school, we want you to succeed in your earthly school, and we are doing everything we can to preserve you and your school. As I have just explained, many of us have gone so far as to reincarnate in a human body to assist you. This is no small intervention, and it isn't done without potential consequences to those who volunteer to do this.

Some Star People get lost for quite some time in the human condition before they wake up out of it, and that is painful, as you well know. And some do not succeed in their mission: They wake up, but for any number of reasons, they are unable to fulfill their mission. That is also painful. And some don't manage to wake up at all during that lifetime. *And* there is no guarantee that our overall intervention will work sufficiently to make a difference. You may see us as all-powerful, but once we become human, we have all the limitations that you do.

Yes, Star People have special gifts—psychic gifts, healing gifts, intellectual gifts, and other unusual talents—that most humans don't. But because psychic gifts and other unusual talents are often not understood or accepted by conventional society, Star People are often disparaged and not taken seriously. Not surprisingly, they often find it difficult to gain positions of power. Being unconventional and having special gifts in your society is not a particularly easy path to walk.

Star People need influence in society to make the changes they came to earth to make, but they are sometimes the last to have influence. This is one of the more difficult issues Star People face: Star People and their ideas and inventions are often not very credible to conventional people. They seem far out. And their ideas *are* far out—so far into the future that others can't relate to them. To many, their ideas seem crazy and impractical, while they are the key to your problems. Star

People need those who are more conventional to back them financially and help them get their solutions out into the world.

Some of you have fantasies that ETs will save you with their technology, and they will, but not in the way you might think. ETs and other higher dimensional beings like ourselves are sending you the information you need through Star People, through dreams, through visions, and through your intuition. This is the intervention. This is how you will be saved. You will save yourselves.

ETs are helping you from higher dimensions, just as we are. But it has become increasingly clear that actually appearing to you *en masse* would be highly disruptive, so that is a less likely scenario than we once thought. We are playing this by ear, so that may still happen.

You might think you are ready for this, but we see clearly that you are not. A mere belief in the existence of ETs is not enough to be ready to meet one. A certain psychological and spiritual level of preparedness has to be reached before this will happen. Humanity is not there yet.

This need not be a problem. Plenty of Star People have awakened to the level they need to, to accomplish their life purpose, and many more will awaken. For the most part, the awakening that is happening today is an awakening of the Star People, not your usual enlightenment process. This is why you see so many making leaps in consciousness and awakening without a spiritual background or history of meditation. And many are being *born* awakened and psychically gifted. The Star People phenomenon explains the burst of higher consciousness on this planet, which those of you on the spiritual path are well aware of—and you just might be one of them!

I want to emphasize that however long it takes for you to awaken is the right experience. Each of you has a unique path, and it isn't helpful to compare yourself or your unfoldment to others. You will likely reach the level of enlightenment that will best serve your life purpose. As I said, not all Star People will become fully enlightened, and many will continue to appear quite ordinary. And that is the right experience.

The voice in your head will compare you with others, but it doesn't know anything about your spiritual path or your spiritual growth. The voice in your head will nearly always tell you that you fall short compared to others. Or if you have a special spiritual experience, it will make you feel special and better than others. Whatever the mind has to say about your spiritual growth, forget it! It can be nothing more than a lie or a misunderstanding.

∞

There is another challenge that all of you on the spiritual path need to be aware of, which is more sinister than your own ego, and it also uses the voice in your head to communicate with you. What I'm speaking about are negative nonphysical beings, including astral beings, demonic beings, and negative ETs, who are trying to interfere with this burgeoning consciousness on planet Earth. These negative beings would like nothing more than to take you down or slow you down, to interfere with your unfoldment and life purpose.

You might assume that spiritual people would be protected from such negativity, and they often are because of their positive vibration. But if you are struggling in your life or if you fall into negativity even briefly, you are still vulnerable to influence from these entities.

So, let me say a little more about them so that you understand the situation better. In this case, knowledge is power, and ignorance is *not* bliss. Negative nonphysical beings have always been part of the human experience, just as positive nonphysical beings, like us, have. The existence of negative beings is not cause for alarm, but it is important that you know about them, or you will be more likely to fall prey to them.

When the voice in your head becomes hateful, exceptionally unkind, degrading, and suggests violence or suicide, it is likely to have been taken over by negative entities. The usual voice in your head, the ego's voice, on the other hand, feels like your own voice and is often quite upbeat. Although the ego's voice judges and pushes you and criticizes you at times, it is just as often a harmless, friendly, chatty voice.

The voice of negative entities is more demonic in tone than your ego's voice and, therefore, more compelling because it stirs up fear and other emotions. Extremely negative thoughts are very hard to ignore! It is also the voice of depression, as most people who are chronically depressed are in the grip of negative entities. This voice is not just your worst self but the worst possible version of a human. It is what some call evil.

The most important thing to understand is that this very negative voice, as unpleasant as it is, cannot actually harm you. It has no power whatsoever to cause you harm—unless you believe it and allow it to influence your actions, in which case *you* would be causing yourself and others harm. I tell you this to empower you, since the only power negative entities have is the power to scare you, make you feel bad, or cause you to behave in harmful ways, and that can only happen if you believe what the voice in your head is saying.

Not believing this voice can be challenging because it can be very convincing, and that is the power it has. But you must realize that this voice is not *your* voice or *your* thoughts, and it doesn't speak the truth. If this voice were coming from someone outside yourself, you could more easily see its falseness and dismiss it. But because this voice is within your own mind, it automatically seems true. This is why it is important to know about this phenomenon. Knowing about negative entities will help you turn away from this voice.

There is more you need to do than turn away, however, because that won't be enough. If you are experiencing this level of evil in your own mind, you need to tell the entities that they are no longer welcome and that they must leave.

If you say this with firmness, but not in anger or fear, they will leave, at least for as long as you remain firm about this and don't go back to the negative thoughts and emotions that allowed them entrance to your energetic field.

Staying positive in thought, word, and deed is extremely important. Keeping your vibration positive will keep you clear of negative entities, who would otherwise try to bring you down. With even a small opening, they can take hold and bring your vibration down to theirs.

When this happens, you need to do something about this. Sending any entities away is the first step. Then, take some time to look at the thoughts you were buying into that brought your vibration down. What negative thoughts were you just entertaining?

Nearly everyone has psychological complexes or issues that need to be healed, which become reflected in the voice in your head. When you believe those negative thoughts, then that complex is reinforced, and your vibration is lowered. When these complexes are healed, those thoughts may still show up, but because you no longer believe them, they remain in the background, and your vibration is not affected.

Whenever you disengage from a negative thought, you are saying no to that thought and choosing to stay positive. And whenever you engage with negativity, you are saying yes to that thought and choosing negativity. If you stay involved with that negativity long enough, that is an invitation to negative entities to come close and stay.

Whenever you find yourself caught in negativity, whether it's coming from the ego or an entity, just notice that and choose to switch your attention to something more positive. Then, ask us for help in healing the emotional complex and sending any entities away. Helping to heal you in this way is one of the things we on higher dimensions do for humanity. Angels, in particular, often step in and remove these entities and coax them into the light.

Please use us in this way. You don't have to address any particular spirit helper by name, just send out a call for help and whomever is most suited to help you will answer your call. This is like a 911 call, but you can use it for even minor emergencies. Please don't hesitate to call upon us.

Learning to be aware of the negativity in your mind and to detach from it, which is what is learned through a practice of meditation, and healing the negativity in your mind by investigating it, which I have spoken about in many of my other books, will clear your mind of negativity and make your thoughts less compelling. Once your thoughts are more positive and less compelling, you will be able to land in the present moment and stay there much more easily. This is the goal of spiritual practices and of the spiritual path: to learn to live in the present moment.

∞

There are hopeful signs for your future. I have already mentioned the many Star People who are working to benefit the planet. But there is another segment of the population that can really make a difference, and that is the children and young people growing up today.

They are growing up in a different world than their parents and grandparents. Because things have already changed so much in their lives as a result of technology, they are much more able to adapt to change and much less likely to follow old conventions. And many are passionate about the environment and other issues of great importance, which those who came before them were unable to solve.

Many young people are Star People with exceptional skills and a real drive to do something about the problems in the world, which are very apparent to them. Most are progressive thinkers and willing to stand up for equality and fairness for all. Many are also unwilling to be involved in the usual wars and shenanigans of your governments. The younger generation will bring a fresh perspective to your world, which it badly needs.

One of the most important things you can do for those growing up now is to teach them to meditate. This can greatly reduce the strength of the egoic mind and the damage it can cause emotionally to themselves and others. This, alone, can change society immensely.

Most adults are carrying around emotional baggage from widespread ignorance about emotions and a lack of understanding about the egoic mind. With better information and education about how emotions are created and how to become free of them, children won't become wounded in the first place. Preventing wounding is much easier than healing from it, which can sometimes take lifetimes. Once this information becomes common knowledge and is taught in homes and schools, many of your emotional problems will disappear, and peace will stand a chance.

I have tried to present teachings that will prevent such unnecessary wounding and suffering. It is my sincere desire to assist humanity in understanding how not to create negativity, including negative emotions. If children can be taught this early on, they will be free to be their best selves from the start.

Essentially, all of your problems and suffering stem from the negative thoughts and emotions that derive from the voice in your head. And yet, so few know even this much. I have come to teach this most basic and important truth through this channel and through others. Please hear me, as what I have to say about this is the answer to your personal problems and to your world's salvation. This teaching is one of the ways I have come to save you. I will say more about this in the next chapter.

Peace will only come to your world when peace is established within each of you. It is time that you see this, that you begin to live what I taught two thousand years ago. Unless enough of you change your state of consciousness, humanity stands little chance of survival. I came then and I come now to teach you how to create peace within yourselves and within your world. The answer is, of course, love. Love is the answer to every problem.

War is not the answer. War is a reflection of the war within you, the egoic state of consciousness, which is at war with itself and at war with others. Hatred starts with judgment and fear. Without these, there would be no war. You fight with those you are afraid of and those you judge as wrong or bad. Your ego sees others who are different as a threat to itself. That very perception creates the conflict-ridden and war-torn reality your world is experiencing, and that cannot change until a majority of you stop perceiving life though the ego's eyes.

The ego's way is not love's way, and the ego's perceptions are not the truth. Others will always be different because everyone is unique. If you let differences scare you or cause you to be judgmental, you will forever be in strife. It is the ego that is scared and judges. But you are not the ego.

You can just as well find the love that is within you. You can transcend your fear and judgment by transcending the voice in your head, which is the voice of fear and judgment. If it weren't for that voice, you could live in harmony with your fellow human beings. You are lovers at your core, not haters, not fighters. You do not need to solve your problems through conflict.

War doesn't solve problems. War *is* the problem. It is the manifestation of a misunderstanding inside yourself about what works and doesn't work in life. Your ego believes that fighting with others works, that intimidating and showing force will get you what you want or keep you from losing what you have. But that is mistaken, and it is the opposite of what I taught. I taught love. Love is what works. And the fact that war is not working in your world should tell you something: Your thinking is flawed.

The problem is that you don't trust love enough to choose that instead of war. You don't trust love—but you haven't tried it. Governments keep trying to change things in the world in the same ineffective ways they always have—through war and intimidation. It's time for a change. As I said, after two thousand years, it's time to put what I taught into action.

What would that look like? Essentially it would look like this: Instead of nations investing in a military, they would give others what was needed to raise them from poverty to self-sufficiency. That might be food, educational opportunities, healthcare, contraception, assistance in building infrastructure or starting businesses, or any number of other things.

The unequal distribution of wealth and resources is the problem. Without that, you would work out your ideological and religious differences. For instance, if the United States were to give radicalized Muslims resources to uplift themselves, how could they continue to hate you, no matter what their different beliefs are?

They hate you because they see you as the enemy, and they have their reasons for that. If you are no longer seen as the enemy, they have no reason to go to war with you. How can you befriend and help your so-called enemies rather than fight them? What do they want from you that you could give them?

Going from the way your world is now to this more ideal world must seem impossible. How is this accomplished? Fortunately, there are many intelligent people in the world today who know how to do this. The biggest hurdle is convincing people that this is the way forward, that peace and love are the way. The principle is simple: When you give, you receive back in kind. Everyone wins with love. This is how the world will come together, and it is the only way that it will.

Chapter 3

Being Human

The first thing I want to say about being human is that you are *not* human. This is important. You see yourselves a certain way, but that is not the whole truth. You are human, but you are not *only* human. Or, it would be even truer to say that you are temporarily experiencing being human, but you are not essentially human.

You are divine, as is every creation. Every creation has its origin in divinity. Every creation comes from God, and every creation returns to God. In between, for a while, your soul is experiencing what being human on earth is like. Your soul might also have already experienced being a humanoid on some other planet. And perhaps you will experience that the next time you reincarnate, if you do.

Life is an adventure for your soul. Being human on earth is but one chapter of that adventure, one brief chapter. My point is that you are the Divine masquerading as a human, and so is everyone else. The Divine is infinite, eternal, omnipotent, and omnipresent, and it manifests as all of creation. It lives within creation. So, the Divine that is in you is in everyone and everything. The same consciousness is within everything, although the physical form through which it expresses shapes the experience of the Divine in that corner of the universe.

Every creation offers the Divine a unique, an interesting, and an ever-evolving perspective. The Divine has a different experience as a frog than it does as a butterfly or a dolphin or a human. It sees differently, it feels differently, and it has different capabilities and challenges in each of these forms.

This is fun for the Divine. This is interesting for the Divine. Imagine being able to experience anything you could imagine! That is the experience the Divine is having. It is experiencing every possibility through creation, not just every possibility on earth, but every possibility throughout all the universes. That's a lot of experiences! This is what God does: God creates, God lives, God experiences, and God evolves through those experiences. God is inside it all, enjoying it all, and learning from it all.

This is what I most want to impress upon you: You are not really human, not only human. Please remember this. The difference between those who are awake or enlightened and those who are not is that they have realized this, and this sense of being divine is always with them. They are aware that it is the Divine that is looking out of their eyes and using their body and making choices. It is the Divine that feels love, gratitude, awe, peace, contentment, and experiences beauty everywhere.

To the Divine, all of life is beautiful. It is a gift. It is sacred, for it sees itself in everything and loves itself in everything. That is who you are. You are that which experiences life that way.

Being human is very different from that, as you well know. You see, you feel, you experience, you even love, but always there is a sense that something is not right, something needs fixing, and you can't just relax and be. You feel like you are flawed, your life isn't what you want it to be, your spouse isn't what you want him or her to be, your work isn't enjoyable, even your children are not so enjoyable. Nothing is ever good enough, at least not for long.

That is the human lens, and believe me, it is just a lens, a pair of glasses that colors and distorts life, making life seem unpleasant, like a funhouse mirror that isn't so fun. That experience of being human doesn't have to be your experience. When you shift the lens from which you look, everything changes. When you see with your divine eyes, life as a human being is good: It's a marvel, it's a wonder, it's beautiful, and it's precious. Such a gift—to be able to experience life as the Divine in a human body. That is the goal of your earthly lifetimes.

The goal of my teachings is to help you do that, to help you transform your perception from human to divine while you are in this human lifetime. To do that, I will have to describe to you more specifically what makes you human, that is, what makes you complain and be unhappy, feel lacking, wish there were more, wish you were different in some way, and be unkind. I will have to tell you about the ego.

The ego is the programming that makes you unhappy and dissatisfied. The ego is just programming; it isn't an entity, as many imagine—a little *you* inside your head—although it feels like that at times. The ego is the programming that shapes what the voice in your head says to you. By examining the voice in your head, you can get to know the ego.

This programming provides a way of perceiving life. It is a viewpoint—the ego's viewpoint—and that viewpoint is deeply flawed. The ego doesn't see life as it truly is. You are programmed to misperceive life. And you are programmed to try to fix what you perceive by doing and getting rather than by *being*: by looking within yourself and discovering what is actually true and, thereby, releasing yourself from the suffering caused by the ego's misperceptions.

The ego is the programming that creates unhappiness and then offers solutions to that unhappiness. The problem is that the solutions don't work, at least not for long, not to mention that this programming is the cause of your suffering in the first place. Without the ego, you would be happy and content and kind to each other. The way to happiness, contentment, and love, therefore, is to see the truth about the programming, to see that it is false.

Seeing the truth about it is tricky, though, because you are programmed to believe your programming. Your programming seems true, and it is ingrained, automatic, and compelling. Your programming is very convincing! To discover the falseness of your programming, you have to be willing to examine it and question it. This is no small order; it can be quite scary to take this step. Questioning your programming is like questioning your very foundations. Questioning the programming puts you on shaky ground. What will happen to you if you do?

But to become free of the programming, much more is needed. It isn't enough to just be convinced that your programming is false, because the programming is still operating in every moment. The programming doesn't stop just because you have learned the truth about it. It continues as it always has.

For the programming to stop or not run you anymore, it has to be disassembled piece by piece. The false beliefs produced by the programming have to be seen as false, one by one, moment to moment. That is the work, and this is bound to take time.

This work requires that you be aware of the thoughts that run through your mind. And even that is not enough, for you also have to see that those thoughts are false and stop believing them. Then, there's one more thing you have to do: Turn your attention to the present moment instead of the voice in your head. So, breaking free from the programming involves four things:

1. Understanding that the voice in your head is the cause of suffering and that it is not your voice but the voice of your programming (that's the easy part),

2. Becoming aware of the thoughts in the thought-stream, which I've been calling the voice in your head. This awareness is developed in meditation,

3. Inquiring into the thoughts in the thought-stream that you still believe until you are convinced that they aren't true, useful, or worthy of your attention, and

4. Turning your attention away from the realm of thought to real life, to the present moment. That ability to disengage from your thoughts is also developed in meditation.

Meditation is critical to this process. Meditation is the antidote to being caught up in the voice in your head and taking on its perceptions. Meditation develops the skills needed to disassemble the programming. Without a daily practice of meditation, the process of detaching from the voice in your head will take much longer, possibly lifetimes. Meditation will accelerate your emotional and spiritual evolution like nothing else.

∞

The programming is only a problem when you believe it. Once you stop believing the thoughts in the thought-stream, the programming will still run in the background to some extent, but it won't feel as true or compelling as it used to. Eventually, many of your usual thoughts will stop showing up or they'll be like whispers that have no power whatsoever to influence you. As this process progresses, the thoughts in the thought-stream become more benign, and neutral and positive thoughts are not really a problem, although they can still keep you from being more present in your life.

The problematic thoughts are the negative ones: the "I'm less than" and "I'm not okay" thoughts and the "I can't stand this" thoughts. These are never true. Negative thoughts are never true. Just let this sink in. All negative thoughts are part of the programming, not part of the truth.

The truth about life and about yourself is very good news. Life is good; you are good. Anything that tells you otherwise belongs to the programmed lies that make you and everyone else unhappy. You are meant to be happy! You don't need to suffer. Stop believing the voice in your head's lies, and you will experience the truth about yourself and about life.

The truth is hidden from you by lies. The programming is manufacturing the lies that make life seem more unpleasant and scarier than it actually is. It manufactures lies that make you suffer. I will give you a few examples:

❖ The voice in your head tells you that certain things you don't like shouldn't be happening, when they *are* happening. It is a lie to say that something shouldn't be happening when it is. Whatever is happening is happening and, therefore, logically *should* be happening. Believing such lies creates anger, sadness, and sometimes fear when there is no need for these emotions.

Who says that something shouldn't be happening? The ego. It resists the way things are; it fights against life. Being at war with life is unpleasant. If you didn't believe such thoughts, you wouldn't feel at war with life and experience the negative emotions that are part of that, such as anger, sadness, and fear. These emotions are no small matter. They not only make *you* miserable, but also those around you. These emotions are behind every conflict in human affairs, all because something isn't the way you *think* it should be.

❖ The voice in your head scares you by listing all the negative things that could happen in the future. Ideas about the future are lies; they belong to an imaginary reality, not reality. These ideas come from the ego, and the ego doesn't have a crystal ball. The ego isn't what is smart or wise about you. The ego is just programming. So much energy and emotion are wasted contemplating negative possibilities. These thoughts don't even protect you; they only make you miserable and keep you out of the present moment.

Your wise self, your divine self, knows how to take care of you and what to do moment to moment to keep you safe. If you stay present in the moment, you will know what's best to do in any situation that might come up. However, if you are busy strategizing about future possibilities or lost in thought for other reasons, you won't be present. Instead of your divine self being in charge, the ego will be, and the ego isn't nearly as wise.

❖ The voice in your head makes up stories—lies—in an attempt to define you. The voice in your head tells you who you are through all the thoughts that start with "I." Most of these stories make you feel bad. They often paint a picture of someone who is limited, lacking, or not good enough. Even the ones that are meant to make you feel superior leave you feeling separate from others, which doesn't feel good either. Even if there is *some* truth in these stories, they are lies because they are not the whole truth.

These negative stories drive people to overwork and stressfully strive toward some impossible ideal in an attempt to prove these stories wrong and become happier. Then, to cope, people often overeat or overindulge in some other way. These stories drive addictions, wreak havoc with relationships, and make you miserable. Who would you be without these stories? How would life feel without these stories?

❖ The voice in your head generates all sorts of unnecessary desires, which if not obtained, create suffering. It's natural to have desires and preferences. For instance, it's natural to want freedom, love, peace, and happiness. Those are desires that stem from your divine nature. But the voice in your head wants other things, less essential things, including frivolous things and clearly unattainable things. Not attaining what the ego wants results in sadness, anger resentment, jealousy, and other unpleasant emotions. Without those desires, you wouldn't experience those feelings.

The ego's desires are lies: Who is the "I" that wants? That "I" is a lie. It doesn't point to a real person, only an idea of a person. You are not that "I." The proof is that you are able to notice this "I" and think about it. Who is it that can observe and think about the "I?" That is who you really are.

And what is the implication in having the desires of the "I" met? That is also a lie. Embedded in the ego's desires is a lie: the lie that getting those desires met is important to your life and happiness. Happiness doesn't come from getting your ego's desires met, but on connecting with the divine self's love, peace, and joy. That is the truth. Find the happiness that doesn't depend on getting or having but on just being.

❖ The voice in your head dwells on the past, and the past that it dwells on is a lie. Your memory of the past is not the past. Your memory is a mental fabrication. What good is it? And yet, your thoughts about the past cause so much suffering: your regrets, your painful memories, your longings for the past—all unnecessarily painful. Without your memories of the past, you wouldn't suffer over the past. Without these lies, you wouldn't suffer.

Your memories seem to be true and seem to be valuable, and that's also a lie. You don't need your thoughts about the past. The painful memories make you sad, and the happy ones take you out of the present moment and make you long for something that no longer exists. It hurts to want something that isn't in your current experience. Thoughts about the past cause you pain or, at the very least, take you out of the present moment, no matter what they are.

❖ The voice in your head judges, and judgments are also lies. The ego's judgments are lies because they pretend to be wise and all-knowing. But the ego is neither of these, so how can its judgments be? The truth is, the ego has no wisdom, it pretends to know things it doesn't know, and you are neither superior nor inferior to anyone else, as your judgments assume.

Your judgments seem important, true, and useful, but they are not. That is the illusion, the lie. You are programmed to believe that lie—that your judgments are true and valuable—so naturally you believe your judgments.

You are programmed to believe all the lies the ego tells you through the voice in your head. But it's time to wake up from this illusion, from the false perceptions you have been programmed with, and to see the truth. The truth is, all your judgments do is make you and others unhappy. They are behind conflict on every level, including between nations and religions.

❖ The voice in your head, the ego, tells you what's good and bad, and these assessments are lies. Such evaluations aren't based on essential moral truths but, rather, on the ego's assessment of what's good or bad for "me," good or bad for Number 1.

The problem with this is that the ego doesn't see the whole picture. Its perspective doesn't include what's good or bad for others or for the Whole. The ego's perspective leaves out so much. Because the ego's evaluations are short-sighted and self-centered, they are lies. And they are lies because they are not in alignment with the truth: with the truth of who you are, with the truth about the Whole, or with the truth about life. The ego's ideas about good and bad are not a good compass for how to live your life.

If you believe the lies of good and bad, your life becomes all about getting what is deemed good and avoiding what is deemed bad by the ego. The ego is not a worthy arbiter of this. This is not what life is about. It is about love: learning to love and *being* love. About that, the ego knows nothing. What the voice in your head has to say about love is not trustworthy.

Believing lies always makes you suffer. You suffer when you believe something is good and you don't get it, or something is bad and you do get it. Believing the ego's assessments of good and bad sets you up for unnecessary disappointment and unhappiness, and it leads to an empty and unfulfilling life.

∞

Dear ones, I hope you understand that you are not this unhappy, discontent, and unkind voice in your head. Then, once you know that, you can begin to see what else is here, which has always been here but has allowed you to believe that you are what the voice in your head says you are until you are ready to discover the truth about who you *really* are. Discovering this truth is like finding out that you are the heir to a beautiful kingdom when you believed you were a pauper.

The truth is such good news, and it isn't really that hidden. Who you really are is what has been alive and experiencing your life all along. It is what sees, hears, tastes, smells, and senses life. It is what loves life, what laughs, what has fun, what is curious, what is strong and courageous, what is kind, and what is good. Every time you express curiosity, strength, courage, wisdom, love, kindness, playfulness, compassion, goodness, and light-heartedness, that is your real self—your divine self—peeking out from behind the ego.

Your divine self is also what allows identification with the ego to happen. It allows getting lost in thought to happen. It allows the ego—the programming—to run the show until you—the you that is awakening from the egoic trance—are ready to see the truth.

You see, it is not a mistake that you are run by the programming and become lost in the illusion. There's a time for everything: Just as there is a time to believe you are the ego and act that out, there is a time to discover that you are *not* the ego and find out what living as that is like.

Every stage of life is good, as it is meant to be, and right on schedule. You are unfolding as you need to and as divinely intended. You can relax and let yourself be taken to this next, beautiful phase, which is free from the suffering you have experienced in the past.

Since you are reading this, it must be time for you to awaken or for you to, at least, begin to awaken. If you are open to these words and able to see the truth in them, then you are ready to see the falseness of the ego and break free of it. This is the time, and there is no better time, because the world needs you to see life through a more loving, kind, and peaceful lens.

Being human is difficult for another reason besides your own ego: Being human is difficult because of other people's egos. Even if you are no longer tied to your ego and the voice in your head and you are able to act and speak from a more loving place, the people around you are likely to still be tied to their egos. It isn't enough for you to be free from your ego if most other people are not; the vibration of humanity will remain dense. Those who are awakened must find ways to affect others, to raise their vibration.

This happens naturally to some extent through a transmission of energy: If you are in a higher consciousness, those around you may be uplifted without them even being aware of it. That is Grace. In this way, you are a beacon of light in the darkness. Your light shines on and lights up those around you. Unfortunately, the opposite can be true: Your vibration may be lowered by the vibration of others if you aren't careful.

Today's world is very dense vibrationally. Humanity's overall state of consciousness is quite low, and that state of consciousness has shaped the world you live in and how people behave. Most people's lives are busy, fast-paced, competitive, and stressful. Many are vying for basic resources and just trying to survive, while those who are more affluent are competing for even more money, power, status, and recognition.

Your world is essentially a reflection of the egoic state of consciousness. Most people are deeply identified with their egoic minds, the voice in their head, and have very little awareness that another way of living is possible—another way of *being*. And Christianity hasn't helped the situation.

Christianity doesn't offer a vision of another way of being in the world, even though I was an example of that, or even suggest that a different experience of life is possible, except in heaven. Christianity would have you accept your so-called sinning nature and that suffering is your lot until you get to heaven. Christianity also does a poor job of explaining the suffering in life.

Christianity doesn't assume that people can substantially improve their state of consciousness except perhaps by praying or going to confession or doing good works. Christianity has little to say about achieving a higher state of consciousness, except acknowledging that a few saints have done so, but without much of an explanation about how this was achieved.

When I walked the earth, I lived in a higher state of consciousness, and I knew about raising consciousness. I practiced meditation and taught my disciples and others close to me what I had learned about meditation and higher states of consciousness while traveling in India. My teachings then included esoteric and metaphysical truths, but those deeper truths were lost. The "how-to" for the common man or woman—how to reach higher states of consciousness—was lost. And this is what is missing in Christianity.

This is a rather profound failing in the Christian church. The church fathers didn't want parishioners to know that they could reach the higher levels of consciousness that I had reached. And, to be fair, most church authorities simply didn't know this was possible. Higher states of consciousness were not in their experience, since they had never received the esoteric teachings that would make this possible for some. How can you teach something you don't know? So, Christianity was bound to be lost to pomp and circumstance, to rituals that would never lead to true transformation but perhaps only raise people's hopes of a better life in heaven after death.

No, the church did not and does not teach that you have the same divine potential that I had. And I wish to correct that. Many in the West are now open to and ready for this message, thanks to the infusion of Eastern ideas into the West since the 1960s. Esoteric knowledge was not buried in the East to the extent that it was in the West, and I am thankful for that.

In the East, transmission of consciousness, or energy, was well understood and practiced between guru and disciple. Disciples didn't just receive teachings from the guru but something else very precious: a transmission of consciousness. They were uplifted by being in the guru's presence. They were given a taste of the guru's consciousness, a taste that may not have lasted, but a taste nonetheless.

The transmission of a higher state of consciousness from a guru or spiritual teacher is a great gift, and it is the most effective means of helping aspirants achieve a higher state of consciousness. The spiritual teacher shifts the student's brain state for them, which is also what happens in meditation, and that is the beginning of the student becoming more established in that higher state.

A higher state of consciousness can only really be known by experiencing it, since words cannot adequately describe it or convey it. The experience of it *is* the teaching, and the rest of the teachings are about how to reach that higher state and what it's like to live in it.

These are the important teachings, which were not included in what I was said to have taught two thousand years ago. This was a great omission. I was revered then not only because people recognized the truth in the simple teachings I presented, but also because they received a transmission from me and were uplifted in my presence. They felt better in my presence.

Once I was no longer alive, all that was left of my teachings were relatively few words, most of which were designed to teach people how to behave, not raise their consciousness. The problem is that you can't get to a higher state of consciousness through good behavior alone, although good behavior helps and is important. And it will be difficult to be good consistently without a shift in consciousness. First things first. People *try* to be good all the time and fail because they are still in the grip of their egos. But once your consciousness has shifted and you are beyond the ego, good behavior is natural. Good behavior follows from higher consciousness, not the other way around.

The point I want to make is that spirituality is about your state of consciousness; it is not about beliefs or rituals. Spirituality is about raising your state of consciousness and living in a way that is aligned with your divine self rather than your egoic self. It's about seeing through a new lens and living in a new way, one that is no longer determined by the voice in your head and the ego's drives and desires.

∞

Your state of consciousness matters, not just to you, but to everyone around you. Everyone affects everyone else through transmission. Just as gurus and spiritual teachers transmit higher consciousness, everyone transmits whatever state of consciousness they are in. So, when you are living among people who are mostly in a lower state of consciousness, your consciousness will either slide down to match theirs or theirs will slide up to match yours.

What I'd like to explain is how you can keep your vibration high in the midst of others who are in a lower vibration. This can be done, but it is particularly challenging if you aren't seated firmly in a higher state. So, that is the first issue: becoming more firmly established in a higher state of consciousness. This takes time and practice. Moving into a higher state of consciousness in meditation is not so difficult; many have mastered that. But remaining in that state outside of meditation proves not to be so easy, and understandably so. It is not easy to maintain a higher state of consciousness in this world. So here are some suggestions for doing that:

❖ Take time each day to meditate at least an hour every day, in one sitting, at whatever time of day you prefer. Do this in a comfortable position so that you can meditate for this long without discomfort. I've explained the basics of meditation in other books, so I won't detail that here. And this author has online courses that teach meditation. Daily meditation is the most important thing you can do to support your spiritual unfoldment.

❖ When you are with people, instead of talking, listen as much as possible. What I mean is listen to what people are saying and also listen to—or notice—the voice in your head's thoughts without giving voice to them. Try to listen to others with your Heart, the spiritual Heart, without filtering what they are saying through your mind's judgments and opinions.

Listening with your Heart is being receptive to what *is* without evaluation: accepting the way things are and the way people are, with curiosity, allowing, and compassion. This is what your divine self is always doing. However, you won't be able to be this way with people if you are busy listening to the voice in your head and expressing those thoughts.

When you are with others, drop out of all thoughts and just be and receive life as it is happening. Let others have their judgments and opinions without jumping in and agreeing or disagreeing with them. Practice letting everything and everyone be as it is and as he or she is. Your experience of life and of them will be very different than if you join them in their ego's world of constant evaluation and likes and don't likes. Notice how relaxed you feel when you are being with others this way. What a difference this is from the egoic state of consciousness!

You might be concerned that others will think you are odd if you are silent much of the time, but you are likely to discover that, in this state of just being, you are more likeable and attractive than ever!

❖ When you find yourself stressed out, rushing around, confused, or caught up in the voice in your head, just stop. Stop whatever you are doing and focus on taking some slow, deep breaths. Breathe in slowly and deeply from your diaphragm to the count of six and then breathe out slowly to the count of six. Do this for ten minutes, and then check inside yourself and see what's true to do next.

You get to choose how you live your life. You don't have to let the default, the egoic mind, determine what you do and how you do it. Don't let the voice in your head, which is the voice of stress, run you or determine your actions. Instead, let joy determine what you do next.

What do *you* want to do now? What do you need? Maybe you need to stop and rest a little longer than ten minutes. Maybe you need to stare out the window and just *be* for a while. Let yourself just *be* until you are clear how your deeper self wants to move you next.

If you let the voice in your head run you, it will run you ragged, until you are exhausted and cranky, and that is no way to live. And yet, that is a description of how many do live their lives. Then, they make it up to themselves, supposedly, by overeating or overindulging in some other form of pleasure.

There's another way, and that is to balance your activity with rest and just being. This may sound impractical, but being stressed out and unhappy is not a very functional or effective state. You can choose to be more balanced about how you go about your day by periodically stopping what you are doing and checking inside yourself and asking, "Where is my joy now? What am I being moved by joy to do or not do now? What is true to do now?"

You may find that when you let your divine self determine your activities, some activities will naturally fall by the wayside, as they will be recognized as unworthwhile or unnecessary. The ego makes things that are unimportant important, which is one way it keeps you unnecessarily busy.

Busy-ness is the name of the game for the ego, for it loses all power when you just stop and let yourself be. Find out what activities come out of just being by just stopping for a bit and seeing. Your divine self knows how to live your life if you give it a chance. However, its directives don't come in the form of words in your head but, rather, in the form of inspiration and urges to act when the time is right for that.

❖ Avoid negative people whenever you can. This is not being unkind—you can still be kind to them; it's being smart and taking care of yourself. Unless you are meant to be of service to someone who is struggling with negativity, then it probably serves no purpose to be involved with that person if it can be avoided. That person's vibration will probably not be raised by yours unless he or she is very open to you, and your vibration could be adversely affected if you engage with him or her.

Avoiding negative people is just good emotional hygiene. Why put yourself in positions that might trigger your issues or activate your judgments and bring down your vibration? This is especially important if you aren't well-established in a higher state. Those who are just learning to be more present in their life would be wise to choose carefully who they spend their time with. Those who are more established in Presence can often hold their own around negative people, but they also rarely choose to be with them unless they are called to be of service to them.

Spiritual people often find it difficult to make this transition to being more discriminating about who they spend their time with because they don't want to hurt anyone's feelings. And sometimes people's feelings are hurt when your relationship with them changes. But such change is part of life, and this simply has to be accepted—by them and by you.

This also goes for family members. Spiritual people feel especially guilty about wanting to spend less time with family members, but that, too, must be accepted by all concerned. You can't let other people, including family members, determine how you live your life. In the end, you must be true to yourself—true to what is true for you in any given moment. If it is not true for you—if you don't feel a yes inside—to spend time with certain family members, then don't, unless it's absolutely necessary. You have only so much time and energy. Where you spend it matters to your consciousness.

❖ Involve yourself in activities you love that raise your consciousness: dance, sing, play an instrument, listen to music, create something, draw or paint, walk in nature, play with your dog, ride your bike or play a sport, read spiritual books or listen to recordings of spiritual books or teachings.

Do what you love and what makes you feel good and happy—and do these things daily. Spend as much time as you can doing things like these that make you happy and keep your vibration high.

These kinds of activities raise your consciousness and make you feel good because they focus your attention on real life, which is brought to you by your senses, instead of on the mind's virtual reality. Even reading spiritual books is a practice of focusing your mind and brings you out of the imaginary reality of "me, myself, and I."

Whenever you get lost in what you are doing, even reading, you drop into your divine self's enjoyment of life. On the other hand, whenever you get lost in your thoughts about yourself and your life, you lose contact with real life and experience the ego's world of lack and discontentment.

❖ Mantras, positive affirmations, and prayers are other excellent tools for maintaining a higher state of consciousness or moving into a higher state of consciousness when you've lost that. Since I've spoken quite a bit about these in my books and guided meditations, I won't elaborate further here.

❖ Surround yourself with beauty and with what brings you joy, and get rid of what doesn't. Beauty opens the Heart, and beauty is very available. Nature makes beauty available to almost anyone. Spending time in nature is one of the most refreshing and consciousness-raising things you can do. Nature is alive, and it doesn't have an egoic mind. For this reason, being in nature is relaxing, and when you relax, you fall into your divine nature. Human beings naturally love beauty and relax in the presence of natural beauty.

Your home can also be a sanctuary for you, a place where you experience relaxation, calm, and beauty. Do whatever you can to make your environment pleasing to you. Your environment is important, and it holds a certain vibration. If you have the TV on a lot, for instance, that will affect the vibration in your home. Since TV tends to be quite negative and violent, it is important to minimize the amount of time you spend watching it. Meditation also affects the vibration in your home: The more you meditate, the more that vibration permeates your home and can help you sustain a higher level of consciousness.

Having things in your home that you love is important. Then, when your eyes land on those things, they spark gratitude and joy. For the same reason, it's important to move things out of your home that you have negative associations with or don't need. Subtly, you react negatively to those things, and they can bring your vibration down.

Your home environment is one thing you have some control over. Make it a peaceful, love-filled space by creating a sense of the sacred within that space. Choose things that reflect or enhance your state of consciousness and get rid of things that don't. Let it be a place where you feel gratitude for everything you own. Do what you can to make your home a place where your divine self is expressed and experienced.

❖ If you want to maintain a higher vibration, it's important that you monitor and limit what you watch on TV and on the internet, including news. For the most part, TV and other media reflect the average state of consciousness, which is quite low. Most people on TV and in the movies are deeply identified with their egos.

TV and movies portray the full range of negative human emotions and usually more intensely than you normally experience them. What you see is people who are suffering and often dealing with that in ways that create even more suffering for themselves and others. You see people caught in negative states of consciousness and acting out negatively. And you often identify with their intense emotions, which is not particularly healthy: When they feel angry, you feel angry; and when they feel scared, you feel scared. If something you are watching causes you to contract energetically, then watching that is not good for you, and it's time to turn it off.

What you have modeled on TV and in the movies is more often how *not* to deal with your emotions than how to deal with them in a healthy manner, since that seemingly wouldn't further the plotline. The characters on TV and in the movies drive the storyline forward through one poor choice after another. They do everything you aren't supposed to do—lie, cheat, manipulate, murder, hurt others—all in an attempt to deal with their own negative emotional state or egoic drives. What you are watching on TV and in the movies is the ego on steroids.

This may seem rather innocent: watching others make worse choices than you would ever make. *Seinfeld* was a genius at showing you the foibles of the ego and the trouble it causes, and it made you laugh. However, what's really happening in this show and much more so in most others is that you are being taught that such egoic behavior is normal. Instead of being shown enlightened models of human behavior, you are being shown the worst of human nature. And although that behavior might not be being celebrated, these shows are still sending a message to your unconscious mind that this is how human beings act, which translates as "it's okay to act this way."

Yes, there are some shining examples of human beings on TV and in the movies, but they are the exception. The models of spirituality that do exist in real life, if they are shown at all in the media, are inaccurately portrayed and made fun of or considered dangerous. Spiritual people are usually depicted as crazy or part of a cult or on the fringe of society.

This constant portrayal of the ego and the worst side of humanity helps keep people in the prison of their ego. It reinforces the negative conditioning that *is* the ego. Your mistaken egoic beliefs are reinforced. For instance, the constant emphasis on women's bodies and beauty reinforces the conditioned belief that this is what is important about a woman, when it's not. This is a very oppressive and limiting subliminal message! Granted, once you are awake to the truth about the ego, the media has less power to reinforce your negative conditioning, but your unconscious mind is still affected to some extent by everything you see.

One of the most damaging things about the media is the fear that it stirs up. It shows every possible terrible thing that can happen, as if these things are a part of everyday life. TV and the movies put violent and tragic images into your unconscious mind, and you begin to believe that life is actually as scary and tragic as these fantastical stories. It is not healthy to believe that life is scary. It is literally unhealthy to be afraid because of the chemicals that are released in the body when you are afraid. Scary movies are not healthy, and certainly not for children, who are just forming their ideas about the world.

The ego perceives the world as scarier than it is, and it gives you all the reasons you *should* be scared. Yes, there are dangers in the world, and you have to be careful, but there isn't a tiger or a terrorist around every corner. If your ideas about life are derived from TV and the movies, which they are to some extent whether you are aware of that or not, then you will find ordinary life quite overwhelming, when it isn't. And you are likely to spend more time worrying unnecessarily about the future than being present in the here and now. These shows don't teach the truth but reinforce the ego's fears, perceptions, and misunderstandings.

But even worse than this is the idea, so often portrayed on TV and in the movies, that violence is the solution to your problems. When you see violent acts on TV, and especially when children do, violence is normalized. People come to see violence as a viable solution to their difficulties, without really understanding the ramifications of a violent act to oneself and to society.

Without such images on TV and in the movies, war would be impossible. These images serve the military-industrial complex. They feed the belief that the way to deal with your enemies is to kill them, which no mother or father would actually teach their children.

Mothers and fathers teach love and respect for others, while taking their children to movies that show conquest, imprisonment, war, and violence. What do you think sinks into the unconscious mind more effectively? I will tell you that images sink into the unconscious mind more effectively than words.

Images go straight through to the unconscious mind, bypassing any rational reflection or evaluation. It doesn't matter what you are telling your children if they are being fed violence on a daily basis. They, like most people on earth, won't believe that peace is even possible. They'll continue to believe that people are incapable of getting along and that there will always be enemies to fight.

You have to begin seeing your fellow human being, no matter what he or she looks like or believes, as a friend, not a foe, or he or she will never be a friend. That is the first step toward peace: You have to change how you perceive others. The ego perceives others as a threat, while the divine self perceives others as itself. This change in perception requires a shift in consciousness.

∞

As I said at the beginning of this chapter, you are not actually human. But you *are* stuck with your human programming while you are here on earth. You can't get rid of it entirely, and you wouldn't want to, since you need some of it, but you can dismantle some of it and also weaken what isn't working for you.

So much of the programming is not working for you. I will give you some more examples of dysfunctional programming, which you would be better off disregarding.

Some of the most dysfunctional and pervasive thoughts in the thought-stream are the ones that begin with "I like" and "I don't like." This may sound funny, since it seems like these are pretty important thoughts. Don't you need to know what you like and don't like?

The answer is that you already know what you like and don't like: You aren't going to eat a lemon instead of an orange, for example. You don't need the voice in your head to tell you, "I like oranges and I don't like lemons," you'll just pick up an orange to eat instead of a lemon. "I like" and "I don't like" are dysfunctional because you don't need them but you think you do. So, you involve yourself with such thoughts instead of just being in the here and now and letting the wise being that you are live your life.

These thoughts, "I like" and "I don't like," are one of the main ways the false self is created and maintained, which is also why these thoughts are dysfunctional. They take you away from your divine self and imply the existence of a false self. Once you are identified with this false self, you often continue to identify with other beliefs, fears, and worries that belong to the false self. "I like" and "I don't like" are seemingly benign and seemingly true statements that act as hooks that draw you into the world and perceptions of the false self, which are false.

There are a number of other thoughts like these that act as hooks, which perpetuate the false self and are, therefore, dysfunctional. This is also true of "better than" and "less than." These words appear to be functional. Don't you need to be able to discriminate between one apple that is better than another, for instance? Or a car that is better than another? Or even an employee that is better than another? Yes, you do, and you can count on your wise, divine self to be able to do this without any extraneous commentary from the voice in your head. In fact, that's what the voice in your head is: extraneous commentary.

Your divine self will naturally choose whatever is best from the possible choices or do research to determine what is best. That's what your intellect is for, which is not the same thing as the voice in your head. The divine self chooses wisely, and it uses your rational mind and intellect to do that.

You don't need the voice in your head to go around evaluating everything: "This is better than that. She is prettier than her. He is smarter than him. That dog is cuter than that one." If you look, you'll see that the voice in your head is in a nearly constant state of evaluation and comparison. It's what the voice in your head does. It keeps you busy with seemingly important evaluations.

These evaluations pass as truth and fact, when they are not. They pass as important, when they rarely are. In fact, many such evaluations are unfounded or simply personal opinions that have no value whatsoever. You believe that your evaluations about someone or something are the essential truth rather than just opinions, when more often than not, they are just opinions, often based on nothing much. The mind just likes to have opinions, and it often just makes up opinions for the fun of it.

No, you don't need most of your evaluations, although there's a place for evaluation in life. It's just that you don't need the voice in your head spouting them at every turn. You already know, instantly, when you look at two apples, for instance, which one might be preferable, at least to the extent that this can be known. Your intelligence knows what it needs to know without thinking about it or talking about it.

Life is simpler without all the conversation going on in your head. The voice in your head is like having an annoying, opinionated companion constantly chatting with you about anything and everything. How exhausting! You don't have to live with all that chatter. It will lessen when you stop believing that those evaluations are important and necessary and you stop giving them your attention.

These preferences and evaluations—"I like" and "I don't like" and "better than"—easily slide into complaints and other negativity, which is another problem. The voice in your head is a negative Nellie. It doesn't just have preferences; it complains. And those complaints create feelings of discontentment, anger, resentment, and other types of negativity. They make you unhappy, and that *you* is your false self. This is why everyone's false self is unhappy. Your thoughts of "I like" and "I don't like," when taken too seriously, can turn you into an unhappy and unpleasant person. This is an insidious and unfortunate result of having preferences and opinions about everything.

Another group of unnecessary and, therefore, dysfunctional thoughts are your thoughts about the future. How much time do you spend thinking about the future? Most people spend a good deal of time lost in speculations about what might happen and what that would be like. These thoughts also seem important and useful. They seem functional. But are they? How often do your thoughts about the future actually help you in your life? If you examine this, you'll see that there is almost no correlation between your thoughts about the future and how your life actually unfolds.

You are under the impression that you have more control over your life than you actually do, and thinking about the future gives you some sense of control, as if thinking something makes it so or thinking can ensure that you will be able to control or handle something in the future.

You are programmed to believe that your thoughts about the future are worthwhile and necessary. You need to examine them until you see that they aren't. Thinking about the future wastes your time and energy and keeps you from being more present in your life.

I'm not talking about imagining what you might need to pack on a trip you are taking. That is a practical use of your mind in relation to an actual future event. Even so, how often have you still not packed the right things for a trip? Life is a lot messier than you would like to think, and a lot of thinking is simply an effort on the part of the mind to try to get it "right."

Some of the most dysfunctional thoughts are thoughts about the past. These also masquerade as important and necessary, while all they really do is shore up the false self. What is the false self? It is the sum total of ideas you have about yourself.

Where do these ideas come from? Most are stories told about something that happened in the past, with you as the center of that story and spun in a way that describes you in one way or another, often negatively but sometimes flatteringly. For example, you went to Paris, and this makes *you* something: a world traveler, sophisticated, lucky, special. It wasn't just a trip to Paris; that event came to mean something about *you*. It contributed to defining the false self, to how you think about yourself.

The meaning you give to the events in your life defines the false self: *You* were treated badly or *you* were your parents' favorite or *you* were always goofing up or *you* were the class clown. You get your identity (who you think you are) from stories about yourself in the past, either ones you tell about yourself or ones that others tell about you. These stories not only define you but confine you, constrict you to seeing yourself narrowly. These stories make you small.

You don't need these thoughts. You don't need to define yourself in any way. The truth is, who you are is a mystery, an ever-changing and complex mystery. Who knows what you will do or say next? This is not set in stone based on your history, although if you believe your stories about yourself and you believe that that is who you are, then your behavior is likely to fall in line with that: You become what you think you are simply because you believe you are that. That's conditioning.

Conditioning is a set of beliefs that can determine your behavior if you let it. Once you become aware of those beliefs and choose to be free of them, then you can discover who you really are. You discover that "I am," without any further description, is the truest definition of who you are. You are much more than any small story you might tell about yourself.

Stories only remain true when you believe them. Becoming free of your stories is what awakening and enlightenment are all about. You awaken out of the false self to a sense of yourself that is free of any story. When you are empty of all stories, you can know yourself as the light being that you are. Becoming enlightened is a process of becoming less and less who you *thought* you were and more and more who you truly are. You become so empty of thoughts that all that is left is light.

Chapter 4

Reality

The ego misperceives life. It imagines the world and life to be other than the way they are. The ego "sees through a glass darkly." The lens through which it views the world is dirty, and that makes the world seem scarier and more challenging than it actually is. The ego is not seeing life as it actually is. The world as the ego imagines it to be is an illusion.

Reality, on the other hand, is how life and the world actually are. When you see with the Divine's eyes, you see the world and life as they actually are. You are dealing with reality, not illusion. The spiritual path is about learning to see with clear, unadulterated eyes, the eyes of a young child whose ego has not developed fully and who has had little conditioning.

When the illusion is stripped away, what is reality like? It's simple. It's *just this:* whatever you are experiencing now without the evaluation or commentary of the voice in your head. It's just sitting wherever you are sitting, breathing however you are breathing, seeing whatever you are seeing, hearing whatever you are hearing, and sensing whatever you are sensing. Reality is experience without thought. Thought creates the illusion, and when thought stops or remains in the background, you experience reality.

In reality, there is no past or future, only now. The Now—reality—is always changing. Like a river that is constantly on the move, the Now is continually giving birth to new experiences, as what *was* unbegrudgingly disappears. The Now brings you new sights, sounds, smells, tastes, sensations, intuitions, inspirations, urges to act, and information. The Now is a flow of ever-changing experience. That is reality.

Your body-mind is the sensory mechanism that is able to register this ongoing, fresh experience. You are God's sensory mechanism, but you are more than a sensing mechanism. You have arms and hands that can affect life and legs that can move through life. And you have free will. You are capable of freely acting upon life, and that's where the fun comes in.

God is having fun playing in life through you. However, sometimes your free will, and even God's will at times, creates experiences that aren't so fun, and then you learn something from those experiences. Whatever happens is fine with God, who doesn't have a preference about what is experienced. God loves learning and God loves a challenge. God loves any experience, even the experience of not liking an experience, which is a common one, since you have an ego.

It's not your fault that you have an ego that creates an illusory experience of reality. God designed the ego to do this so that God could play within this illusory reality. Just like you might enjoy watching a scary movie, God enjoys being scared and being challenged in the ways your ego challenges you.

For God, and for you, the challenge of having an ego is a temporary experience, entered into for the fun of the challenge, knowing all the while that God could not get permanently lost in this illusory reality. That is also part of the design: You are destined, at some point, to see through the illusion created by the egoic mind and remember who you really are. That is the point most of you are at in your human journey. You are discovering the truth about life and about who you really are.

Once you know the truth, even just intellectually, this journey becomes much easier. Once you know something is an illusion, it loses its power over you. Knowing the truth gives you some perspective on it all. It's like seeing light at the end of a tunnel: You can see that there's a way out of suffering and that the way is clear to the light. You breathe a sigh of relief, and everything becomes much easier from that point on.

Knowing the truth helps ease your suffering, but you still have to walk toward the light for some time before you are in the light and knowing yourself as that. While you are still in the tunnel, you continue to be influenced by the ego, but you also begin to experience yourself as the light. You go back and forth knowing yourself as the ego and knowing yourself as the Divine. This back-and-forth can go on for a very long time before you realize that you are not the ego at all but the light. But for a while, you experience yourself as both.

Awakening is when you step out of the tunnel into the light and leave the tunnel behind. The old sense of yourself as small, trapped, and suffering is replaced by a new, more spacious sense of yourself, one that isn't confined by ideas about who you are but is simply the *experience* of who you are. What you left behind in the tunnel were all the ideas about yourself that kept you feeling lacking and unhappy. Without all those ideas, you can experience yourself more purely as the *being* that you are and always have been.

Yes, you have a body-mind, but that is clearly seen as a vehicle for your being to travel in life. Your body-mind isn't who you are. It's what allows you to experience life, but it has nothing to do with who you really are. You are spirit, and you always have been, just like those of us in higher dimensions. The spirit that animates you is no different than the spirit that animates us and everything else that has ever been created. It is the same spirit. There is one spirit in every created being.

Let this sink in. Who you are is no less than or greater than who I am. We are the same, in different costumes, on the same journey homeward but at different places along that journey. Those of you who are Star People are not even at a different place on that journey than I, but just working in this lower dimension for a while before returning to higher dimensions.

There is no better being than you and no worse being than you. It's all the same being in different disguises. This is what you come to realize as you awaken. You realize your similarity with all that is and that all that is, is only different in form, not different in any other way from you, from who you really are.

The illusion is all of the ideas you have about yourself, which is just conditioning, programming. You think of yourself a certain way, and that makes you behave a certain way to some extent. And you have other programming, reflected in your astrology chart, that programs you with a particular personality, drives, talents, inclinations, and life purpose. The only thing that makes you different from another human being, besides your body (your spirit's vehicle), is this conditioning and programming.

Your body and this programming are enough to give you a sense of being a separate self, which is handy and purposeful in living a human life. You are meant to have this programming and the sense of being an individual, or how could you have a unique life and a unique experience of life? That is God's intention in giving you this programming and an ego that provides a sense of being a separate self.

Furthermore, everyone's programming is imperfect and, at times, problematic. No one is programmed for perfection; everyone is programmed for imperfection. It's not your fault that you are imperfect, that you have issues, or that you have wounds to heal or personality flaws to correct.

There is only so much you can do about the programming you have. Even if you work very hard to become the best person you can be, you will still have some flaws, and you will still make mistakes. So please don't think that the goal is to become perfect. It's not. You will never succeed at that. You must let yourself be imperfect and forgive yourself for your imperfections and forgive others for theirs.

This is all purposeful and as it's meant to be. So, there's no point in lamenting or feeling guilty about your particular programmed way of being. You can't be any different than you are; and yet, you are continually evolving and becoming a finer vehicle for your divine self.

Because of this programming and the ego, which is also programming, there is suffering. It is built into life and unavoidable. So, let's talk about suffering for a moment, because it's important that you understand why human beings suffer as they do.

The easy answer is that you have an ego, as I have explained. If it were not for the ego, you wouldn't experience duality but nonduality: Oneness. What I mean by duality is not only a sense of being a separate individual, which the egoic programming supplies, but also a sense that the world has two aspects to it: good and bad. However, in reality, the world or life is nondual, and that Oneness is innately good, since its essence is love.

Duality is conceptual and an illusion: Life seems to be full of opposites, when it actually is not. The mind sees life through a lens of such concepts, which creates an illusory reality. Although concepts are useful for communicating with others, concepts are not real. They don't belong to reality but to the mind's made-up reality. Believing that such concepts are real leads to suffering.

That still doesn't answer the question of why you have an ego that sees life through such a lens. Why did God create an ego that misperceives life and splits it into good and bad? The only possible explanation is that God intended to build suffering into life this way. If you create an ego that misperceives life, those misperceptions are bound to create suffering. Believing lies cannot lead to happiness or freedom but only to unhappiness and imprisonment in a false reality. God created the ego to misperceive life and cause suffering. But, again, why?

This is not so difficult to answer, really. God created an ego that causes suffering because God wanted to experience suffering. Why? Because God can. If you were eternal and could do anything you wanted, you could even explore what suffering is like. If you had all of eternity to experience everything that was possible to experience in reality, why not also explore an illusory reality?

However, God didn't enter into this dimension, where illusion and suffering exist, without a way out. The plan was not to get lost entirely and irredeemably in illusion. So, God built into the human experience a way out of suffering.

That way out is awareness. God made sure to maintain a certain amount of Self-awareness within this dimension. And in case that was lost, God made sure there were others around who were not completely lost in illusion, who had some awareness of the truth.

God also created a kind of internal alarm clock that would wake God up out of the illusion. At some point in everyone's evolution, the Divine in you begins to wake up to the truth. Awareness brightens and begins to see the truth and then finds others who are also awakening or who have awakened.

You are God awakening to your divine nature. That is really good news! You are not a pitiful human being stuck in a world of suffering, as the ego so often feels. That is its reality, but that isn't reality. Reality is much more benevolent than that! Goodness abounds, love abounds, and your earthly lifetimes are but a relatively short break from all that love and light.

On earth, you are challenged to find your way back to love and light after being separated from love for eons. Eons sounds like a long time. Hundreds or even thousands of lifetimes lived in a physical dimension sounds like forever, but it is but a blink of an eye in the greater scheme of your soul's journey.

So much is gained by this foray into this very dense dimension, which could not have been gained any other way. Being alive on planet Earth is a great blessing, and many, many souls are waiting in line for the privilege to come to earth. It is a very special place, where unique lessons are learned and great compassion can be gained.

I know this may not seem to be so from your point of view. I know how hard it can be on earth. But this is where you learn that your internal state means everything to your happiness and success. You are under the illusion that happiness and success lie in getting or achieving something external to yourself, while the truth is that you have had happiness and success all along, in the simple experience of yourself as who you really are.

Can anyone be happier or more successful than God? You are God. God's happiness and sense of life being a wonderful and successful experience is already yours. It is there inside you because God is there inside you.

Stop a moment and just feel this. Can you feel the joy that God feels in being alive, in simply being alive? Can you feel the love that God has for life and for the opportunity your body-mind gives God to be alive? Can you feel God's curiosity and excitement over discovering how this life of yours will unfold?

Like a wonderful movie or novel, God (and you) wonder how this story that is your life will play out. What will be the wins? What will be the losses? The ups and downs? All of it is delicious to the Creator. You can feel all of God's feelings inside you. They aren't the usual emotions, but deeper, more subtle, and truer and more real than any emotion. This is the truth. God is relishing the experience of being you! God is happy and in love with you and all of life. Life is good!

∞

This internal experience—the experience of your divine self is what you are learning to tune in to. This experience is the experience of reality, because it's what is true. It's what God is experiencing through you. You are programmed to experience what your ego is experiencing, but once you break away from that, you can experience the truth. The ego's experience of life is suffering; God's experience of life is joy. To become free of the illusion, nothing has to change in the external world or about life, only your internal experience. You have to learn to tune in to God's experience of life.

The ego is so busy trying to change things in the world and about life in order to feel better. It keeps you busy trying to fix things and get things, but that never gets you there. The ego doesn't know the way to happiness. It can't help you discover the truth. It's what makes you unhappy and hides the truth from you.

You have to stop spending your time chasing your tail. That's what the ego is doing. You have to stop your activities, especially your striving for more and better, in order to make some other choices. Without stopping your activity, it will be difficult to see what's going on — to see the truth — and, more importantly, to experience God within you, since this requires quiet listening and a receptivity that the ego won't choose to engage in.

It's not the ego that searches for the truth or stops and looks within. What does this is the Divine awakening in you. At a certain point in your spiritual evolution, the Divine moves you to do things that will further your waking up to the truth. The Divine inspires you to seek out spiritual teachers and teachings, meditate and do other practices, slow down, turn within, rest, and just be. These are all key to discovering the truth about life and who you are. This doesn't sound so hard or so unpleasant, does it?

The ego resists these activities at every turn. Its resistance is what makes doing these things seem difficult, like a chore, as if just being, turning within, listening to uplifting teachings, and meditating is a chore! The ego is afraid that you won't achieve its goals if you do these things, and that may be true, but you will "achieve" more meaningful things.

It's important that you see these activities as valuable. Resting, just being, looking within, meditating, and absorbing spiritual teachings seem like luxuries or frivolities to your ego. They are counter to your ego's goals, and to the extent that you are identified with your ego, they will seem like a waste of time to you too.

However, there is no other way to move from the illusion to reality than by doing these things. These *are* the path. If you aren't ready to be on the path, that's fine. But if you are, then doing these things is how you need to spend some of your time.

Most of you are interested in doing these things, but how often do you do them? Are they part of your lifestyle or more occasional? Your spiritual life requires a certain lifestyle to support it. The lifestyle of most Americans and of those in most modern countries is determined by the ego, not the Divine. Most people make little room in their lives for resting, just being, meditating, contemplation, and turning within. People often have to get sick or become disabled before they take time for such things, which is often the spiritual purpose of sickness and disability.

Those on the spiritual path may think they can have it both ways, that they can have their fast-paced, stressful life *and* a spiritual life. I'm not saying that progress on the spiritual path is impossible within a busy lifestyle, and certainly spirituality is more important than ever in such a lifestyle, but stress and too much activity and involvement with people will significantly limit your spiritual progress.

This is why people over the centuries have gone on retreat or into monasteries to further their spiritual growth. They do these things because quiet, solitude, and minimal activity make it possible to experience the subtle realm, where your divine self resides. Noise, people, and activity do the opposite.

It is difficult to be in the world and not be affected by the overall vibration of people and places, which is largely egoic, except in sacred places such as churches and temples and nature. It's difficult to keep your vibration high amidst lots of people, lots of sensory stimulation, and lots of activity, which pretty much describes most cities and most work environments.

Some of you will have to decide what's more important to you—your spiritual growth or professional advancement. On the other hand, some of you are meant to be bridges between this busy world and spirituality by being in the world and bringing your higher consciousness and inspiration to it. This is a challenging role. You have to be able to relate to and navigate the business world, while maintaining a higher state of consciousness. Some of you in this role are Star People and quite capable of performing this feat.

Such a transformation of your work structures is key to shifting the overall state of consciousness on the planet. If only people outside of business shift their consciousness, how will those people be able to effect change within businesses? So, while business and the busy world is a challenge to one's state of consciousness, business and the busy world also need higher consciousness and the wisdom and inventive ideas that flow from that.

Even those who are awakened or enlightened need meditation, quiet, solitude, and time to turn within to stay in touch with the divine self, or Presence. Many mistakenly assume that meditation is no longer necessary after awakening, but it is still necessary, or you will slide back into the egoic state of consciousness periodically or more permanently.

People can awaken and then go back to sleep, and one of the reasons this happens is that they don't have a lifestyle that supports awakening. Other reasons are that they were not established in Presence sufficiently before they awakened or they have unhealed emotional issues that keep them tied to the egoic state.

∞

Being awake is a very different state of consciousness than the egoic state of consciousness, and being awake changes your life in many ways. Your activities will naturally change after you awaken, and they usually will have changed before awakening.

Who you spend time with is also likely to change as well as how much time you spend with people. After awakening, there's generally less need to socialize with others and less fulfillment in doing so. Superficial interactions aren't felt to be very interesting or satisfying, and you are no longer looking to others to fulfill certain needs, like a need for attention or approval.

One of the biggest differences between those who are awakened and those who aren't is that those who are awakened are content with life the way it is and with the little things in life. They feel great gratitude for what they have and for what *is*. They don't need to do or get a lot of things or experiences to be happy.

They enjoy little things like taking walks, sitting on the porch watching the birds, and listening to the wind blowing through the trees. And they enjoy the daily tasks of life rather than rushing through them or resenting them because they'd rather be doing something else. This is a big difference!

Not needing life to be other than the way it is for you to be happy leaves you with a lot of time to enjoy life just the way it is. You aren't racing around trying to earn money for something you want or trying to get more than you already have. If you do get more, that's fine, but getting more isn't why you do what you do. You do what you do out of joy, not for some possible future gain.

This is a very different basis for doing and moving in the world. Most people are moved by their ego's desires and drives for more and better things or experiences, while those who are awakened are moved by something much more subtle and fulfilling, which is difficult to describe.

While the ego moves you to do things with thoughts of "I want" and "I like" and "I need" and "I have to have," the divine self doesn't use words in your head to move you but, rather, subtle urges, drives, pushes, nudges, and inspirations: You are just suddenly moved or inspired to do something.

You know what that's like because you honor those urges to act many times a day. Your divine self is alive and well in all of you! After awakening, this way of being and moving through life becomes a way of life, as these inner urges become your prime motivator rather than the voice in your head.

Thoughts may still be there to "do this now" or "don't do that," but you find yourself doing what you are moved to do regardless of what your thoughts are saying. When this happens, it's surprising! You think one thing and find yourself doing another.

It also becomes apparent that, all along, the voice in your head has been telling you things you already know and don't need to be told. It tells you how to do something when the body already knows how to do it. The voice in your head repeats things you've already learned, like a mother standing over a child's shoulder, guiding and evaluating the child's every move. Much of what the voice in your head says falls in this category.

For example, if you are making dinner, the voice in your head might say, "Get the carrots, onions, and broccoli out of the refrigerator" while you are already doing that! And when you are slicing the carrots, it says, "Slicing them the long way would be prettier" and "Be careful!" Then, as you are filling a pot with water, it will warn, "Don't fill it too full." And when the pot's boiling, it tells you, "It's boiling!" Or just before that, it will speculate: "Is it boiling yet?" or "When is it going to boil?" It also comments on how something will turn out, what you need to do next, what not to forget, and how you feel about all of it, including any complaints.

You don't need any of these thoughts. Your body already knows how to make dinner without these thoughts, and making dinner will be much more enjoyable when you stop giving these thoughts your attention. Give your attention, instead, to the sensory experience of slicing carrots or whatever else you are doing, and you will enjoy yourself *and* have access to the wisdom and creativity you need to do this safely and in a way that's fulfilling to you.

After awakening, you just watch the body do what needs to be done, without thinking about it, because the body just knows what to do. That conditioning is already in you, and you don't need it put into words by the voice in your head. You have always been able to live this way, but you thought you needed the voice in your head to tell you what to do and how to do it.

This is a new way of being and doing, in which doing flows naturally from being rather than from thought. Doing bubbles up naturally from the quiet of your being and is executed by the body without a thought. In the egoic state of consciousness, on the other hand, your actions are directed by thoughts and constantly evaluated by the voice in your head.

The ongoing mental commentary that is the voice in your head is largely evaluative and reflective of the duality of the mind: "This is good and that's bad." "I like this but not that."

"You did a better job last time." These thoughts are the stuff of suffering.

Without such thoughts, there's just being and doing and no suffering. Life just is what it is. What you did was part of the flow and couldn't have been different, and now it's done, and life has moved on. How it turned out is how it turned out, and you are on to the next thing. Could it have been better? That question doesn't even make sense from the perspective of the divine self. It is what it is. Period. "Better" is a concept that belongs to duality, and the divine self simply doesn't see things that way.

∞

This brings us to the Heart, the spiritual Heart, your inborn guidance system. Everyone has a guidance system, although not everyone uses it to the same extent. But the Heart is available to everyone. When we, on higher dimensions, guide you, the Heart is the point of contact within the body-mind where our messages are delivered and received. The spiritual Heart is the Divine's command post within the human body and the seat of the intuition, which is the main way spiritual forces communicate with you.

The spiritual Heart is also the seat of all higher emotions, such as love and compassion, which drive you in life, as do your human emotions. However, your human emotions stem from conditioned thoughts and, therefore, belong to the illusory world of the ego rather than reality, the realm of the Divine. Higher emotions, such as love, joy, peace, and compassion, belong to your true nature and don't stem from thoughts. They are ever-present realities, and to experience them, all you have to do is tune in to them.

If you allow these higher emotions to guide you, you will be happy and live a love-filled life. It feels good to follow your joy and do what makes you happy. It feels good to love and to do what you love. It feels good to do what makes you feel peaceful and what brings peace to others. It feels good to be compassionate, generous, courageous, and grateful. These are the higher emotions you have been gifted with, which are meant to guide you through life.

Follow your joy, do what you love, be courageous, be compassionate, and be grateful. This is how to live your life. The other way—doing what the voice in your head suggests—is following the false master, an unwise master, and that can never lead to a fulfilling and love-filled life, since the ego knows nothing about true fulfillment or love.

You are simultaneously human and divine. Your conditioning and other programming runs your human self, while the spiritual Heart enables the Divine to incarnate more fully into the human form. Without the spiritual Heart, you would be cut off from your connection with God. The spiritual Heart is your lifeline, your way back to love, while the voice in your head keeps you tethered to the illusory world of the ego.

To embody the divine self more fully, you have to turn toward the subtle world and away from the voice in your head and tune in to the guidance system you've been given. Following the voice in your head, the default, is the path of least resistance, while what the Heart wants is more difficult to ascertain and takes some discipline to follow, since the ego's messages often compete with and overpower the Heart's messages. You have to learn to follow the Heart, while following the ego is automatic and unconscious.

Then, how or why does anyone ever learn to follow the Heart? The answer is simple: suffering. The ego's way is the way of suffering, while the Heart's way is the way of joy, peace, and love. Following the ego is not satisfying—and worse. It takes you in the wrong direction: toward self-centeredness, endless consumerism and accumulation, dissatisfaction, competition, conflict, and hatred. The egoic state of consciousness is an unhappy place, and every human being wants to be happy. You are programmed to go toward happiness, love, and peace. You are programmed to return Home to love.

Your desire to stop suffering and to be happy drives you to discover the truth about life, which can be known through the Heart. The spiritual Heart tells you what is true and what isn't true for you personally and in general. It tells you this with a simple yes-no guidance system.

When something is true or a good direction for you, the Heart opens, expands, feels joyful and excited, and says, "Yes!" You all know what this feels like even though it's impossible to describe this more fully. The Heart also tells you when something is not true or when a direction is not right for you. Then, the Heart closes, contracts energetically, does not feel excited or joyful, and says, "No."

This all happens in the subtle body and is felt energetically, usually in the center of the chest near the physical heart. Suddenly, you just know something without having thought about it. In fact, thoughts are not part of this guidance system. Although you might think about what you intuited afterwards, that intuition didn't come to you initially in the form of words.

The only exception to this might be if you are a channel and able to receive higher guidance mentally, but that's relatively rare. It's best to assume that guidance won't come to you in the form of words, except perhaps rarely.

You can tell the difference between the Heart's yes and no easily enough, or at least learn the difference easily enough. It isn't hard to know what the spiritual Heart wants and how it's guiding you. But it *is* hard to stay true to it because your egoic mind and other people's can easily dissuade you from following your Heart's guidance.

It's easy to be talked out of following your Heart because there are always reasons to *not* do something. Everything has its disadvantages, and your egoic mind and other people's are quick to come up with those drawbacks. But your ego and other people's egos don't know what's best for you from your soul's perspective.

The Heart's job is to show you what's true for you: your soul's direction. And sometimes there's no rhyme or reason to the Heart. It might guide you to do something that doesn't make much sense to the mind or to others. It might even guide you to do something you don't want to do—something your ego doesn't want to do. When this happens, there will still be a sense of rightness about that choice despite the drawbacks, other people's objections, or your ego's resistance.

You see, there is a plan for your life. It is a general plan; the specifics are not fleshed out ahead of time. But it is a purposeful and meaningful plan for you that has been carefully developed by your soul. The guidance you receive from those in higher dimensions will help you fulfill this plan. There are many different ways it can be fulfilled, and the specific way you do that is up to you. In your Heart, you know your life purpose, although you may not be able to articulate it. You feel it and are drawn forward, mysteriously, to unfold it.

Although you have free will and can go against this plan at any time, your astrological programming makes it likely that you will fulfill your life plan and life purpose in some way. This programming creates drives within you to go in certain directions and not others. It also gives you a personality type that suits your life purpose and lessons. Unlike egoic programming, which can interfere with your life purpose, your astrological programming supports your life purpose. Going against this programming feels unnatural and uncomfortable and often leads to unhappiness and even depression.

The prominent signs in your astrology chart signify certain strengths, drives, needs, and tendencies. Your soul chose to be born at that particular time because that moment in time imprinted you with those strengths, drives, needs, and tendencies.

It isn't that the planets cause you to behave in certain ways. Rather, they represent the energies that were prominent at the moment of your birth, and everything and everyone born at that precise moment is imprinted with those energies. As above, so below: The placement of the planets in the sky represents, or reflects, the alignment of energies that is also present within you in that moment. You are programmed by the energies that were present at the moment of your birth. Astrology is a way of knowing what those energies are and interpreting them.

This is but one of the great mysteries that you are part of, which you understand little about. There is a greater design and a greater plan that operates behind and beyond this universe, which you cannot begin to comprehend.

It would be impossible for you to not be aware of these drives. They are so deeply ingrained in you that you take them for granted, like a fish in water. You just are the way you are. It's easy and natural for you to be the way you are, and you couldn't be any other way. In that sense, your free will is only so free, as your behavior is largely circumscribed and defined by your programming.

These drives operate in the subtle realm. You feel them, but they are more subtle than emotions or sensations. You know what I mean because you experience them. For instance, you may have a drive to write novels or a drive to be a doctor or a drive to work with children or a drive to play music. You are drawn to doing certain things and not others. You love doing certain things and not others. And everyone is different in this regard.

Why do you do the things you do, when others choose to do quite different things? You are meant to do certain things and not others. So, to make yourself do something you don't have a natural drive for would be difficult and unpleasant—and a tragedy from your soul's perspective. Unfortunately, parents often do this to their children because they have their own ideas about what they want their child's life to look like.

The drives I'm speaking about come from deep within, from the Heart, while others, which are common to all human beings, come from the ego. Although the ego's drives don't relate to your life purpose, they are still purposeful, as they bring you the lessons you need as a human being. However, the ego's drives can derail you from the truly meaningful things your soul has in mind for you. The ego's drives and ideas often interfere with the Heart's, and when they do, they lead to unhappiness and even depression.

The ego is driven toward greater comfort, safety, security, superiority, recognition, power, money, and prestige. Pursuing these goals can only bring so much pleasure and happiness, and if pursuing them is at the expense of fulfilling your life purpose, you will surely not be happy.

Putting the ego's goals before the Heart's is like putting the cart before the horse: Your priorities are backwards. But discovering this is one of the lessons of life. Many spend lifetimes pursuing the ego's goals before they realize the emptiness of that. Fulfillment comes from fulfilling your soul's purpose, and you will be pointed toward that by excitement and joy and pointed away from anything that might interfere with that by unhappiness and depression. These are the carrots and sticks in life that help guide you toward doing what you came here to do.

∞

Now, I'd like to touch on another subject related to following your Heart and deserving of further exploration. That subject is how choices are made. Obviously, you are free to choose between anything your mind can think of. The mind offers you plenty of choices when trying to make most decisions. The mind is good at coming up with possibilities. That's its job.

But what winnows down these possibilities? Often that is also the mind, and therein lies the problem. The problem is not that the mind comes up with lots of possible choices; the problem is that most people let the mind make the final choice instead of their Heart.

The most challenging thing about having to make a choice is the pressure you feel around making it. Not knowing what to choose is uncomfortable! The answer to the discomfort is to make a choice, which is what the egoic mind pushes you to do. If you let it, it will make a choice as quickly as possible, since any choice will do to alleviate the discomfort. The problem is that not any choice *will* actually do, not from your soul's perspective anyway.

There are many choices you make that don't matter to the soul, and then whatever you choose leads wherever it leads, and that's fine with the soul. The Divine loves all kinds of experiences and is interested in having any experience.

People are often very concerned about making the wrong choice, when in most instances, there is no wrong choice. They assume that every choice is significant and meaningful, when it isn't. The idea that a choice is either right or wrong is part of the ego's dualistic way of perceiving life, which often ties people in knots unnecessarily when it comes to making choices.

Making the so-called right choice is a challenge for the ego, which feels like it has to be right all the time, as if life is a game and each move has to be played just right — or what? Fear drives this need to always be right, since being right gives the ego some sense of control in a universe where there is little. But what is right, anyway? This is defined by the ego, and it doesn't know. This is just a game the ego plays with itself: the game of right and wrong.

However, some choices do matter to your soul. Some choices will take you in a direction counter to your soul's intentions, and then your soul must communicate this to you some way. There are several ways your soul can do this. First, it works through the spiritual Heart, sending you messages of "no" through subtle and not-so-subtle feelings that convey "no."

For instance, you might feel a sinking feeling in your stomach at the thought of that choice. Or you might feel a sense of heaviness, disappointment, or repulsion. Repulsion is a good way to describe a communication of no from your soul, while attraction is a good way to describe a communication of yes from your soul. You are designed, by God, to go toward what you are attracted to and away from what you feel repulsed by.

If those unpleasant feelings of no aren't heeded, then the soul, through your spirit guides, sends signs that a choice is not aligned with your plan. One way it does this is through messengers: people who discourage you from going in that direction or who have information that might dissuade you from that direction.

If that doesn't work and you are still determined to go in that direction, your soul will create roadblocks, including possibly an illness or accident. One way or another, if you are off-track, your soul will stop you in your tracks if it has to.

The opposite is true for directions the soul wants you to go in: The soul removes roadblocks and smooths the way. Besides making you feel good whenever you think of that choice, your soul will send people your way who support you in going in that direction or give you encouraging information about that direction. Your soul makes the choices it wants you to make easy in any way it can. When a particular direction is important to your soul's plan, things fall into place to support that direction and happen so naturally, smoothly, and sometimes surprisingly that it would seem crazy *not* to say yes to it. Everyone has experienced this.

However, this won't happen with every choice you have to make. This kind of strong and obvious guidance is not given for everything. As I said, not all choices are important to your soul, but they may still be worth making. If you assume something isn't the right choice because fireworks aren't going off when you consider it, you might miss a beneficial opportunity. Not all opportunities are accompanied by a big yes, messengers, and signs, but there will surely be some sense of yes.

As for messages, you have to be careful not to assume that everything you hear from others is a message or sign from your soul. People often get carried away looking for messages and signs outside themselves to tell them what to do.

And please remember that even psychics and channels can be wrong. When a message from someone is coming from your soul, you will feel a sense of joy and rightness in receiving it, while if it's coming from someone's ego, the message won't ring true or feel right.

It's always best to rely on your own intuition, those yeses and nos from the Heart, however subtle they may be. Too many people give their power away to others in the face of a decision and then regret that they did. But that's also one of your lessons as a human being, and it's one that's learned the hard way.

∞

The ego's illusory world is a reaction to reality, which the ego rejects. The ego pretends and makes up a lot of things to placate itself, to make it feel better in the face of a reality it doesn't like and refuses to accept. The ego doesn't like that it doesn't know everything. It doesn't like that it can't control everything. It doesn't like that it can't have everything it wants. It doesn't like that life unfolds as slowly as it does. It doesn't like other people who get in its way or who are different. The ego doesn't like a lot. You could say that the ego *is* resistance to life. It is the programming that resists life.

The ego is also a desirer, and it wants everything now. It is a glutton: It wants and wants and wants some more. It is a desire-producing machine. It churns out one desire after another, as if its desires mean anything in the scheme of things.

Then, the ego is upset when its desires are not met by life. It's angry at life and blames life for not delivering what it wants, as if meeting its desires is the meaning and purpose of life. The ego is egocentric.

From this description, it's obvious that the ego is a primitive—a very young—aspect of humanity. The ego is like a child who believes the world revolves around it, and throwing a tantrum, bullying, blaming others, complaining, manipulating others, and playing the victim is how you get your way in life. These are some of the ego's strategies, and they aren't very good ones, which is why people suffer.

You have a child at the wheel, when you need an adult. Is it any wonder that humanity is still trying to solve its problems through war? Fortunately, there is an adult in the room: your divine self, your rational self.

The ego deludes itself about reality, and that creates the illusory reality it lives in:

In the illusion, the ego imagines getting everything it wants. Those are its fantasies. They are an illusion.

In the illusion, the ego imagines it knows what's going to happen, what should happen, why something happened, what other people are thinking and feeling, and infinitely many other things that it doesn't actually know. Those are its stories, how it makes itself feel superior and more in control than it is and how it calms its fears. Those stories are an illusion.

In the illusion, the ego is afraid. That is the ego scaring itself needlessly. Those fears are an illusion.

In the illusion, the ego imagines that the past is real. That's just one way the ego keeps itself at a distance from reality, from the present moment. Those memories are an illusion.

In the illusion, the ego imagines that it can be perfect. That's just one more frustrating fantasy that makes the ego miserable.

All of these mistaken ideas that make up the illusion cause suffering. Everything that is part of the illusion causes suffering because illusions are lies, and lies cannot lead to happiness.

And that is how it's meant to be. When you are this divorced from the truth, from reality, suffering is the only thing that can wake you up out of the illusion. And that has been the plan all along. When humanity was given an ego, the suffering the ego caused was meant to eventually wake people up from the illusion.

Being lost in the illusion was only ever meant to be temporary—a scary rollercoaster ride that makes you scream with fear and excitement and then laugh once the ride ends. Then, God says, "Let's do that again!" This crazy, unpredictable, beautiful, ugly, wonderful, scary ride called life is its own kind of fun. And if you look within, you can experience, ever so subtly, this sense of excitement and love for life that God feels as God lives life through you.

It will be helpful to take a closer look at the things about reality that your ego and, therefore, you and all human beings have difficulty accepting. Once you see how irrational and futile this resistance is, accepting reality will be much easier.

The first thing to accept is that reality is simple. It's just this: just this moment. It isn't fancy, it isn't a big party, it isn't a big high, it isn't like winning the lottery. It's just this moment. This moment is all you have, and most moments are quite ordinary and simple.

Can you accept this? Is it okay for life to be ordinary and simple? It's not okay to the ego, because *it* doesn't want to be simple and ordinary but very special. That is why the ego doesn't like ordinary. For the ego to *be* special, this moment has to feel special or make the ego feel special. For the ego, everything is about it: How is this for me? What does this mean about me? How am I doing? What's in this for me?

The ego wants every moment to be special, and that is just not how life is—for anyone. This doesn't mean you are not special. Each of you is special. But you don't need a special moment to experience the love within you for yourself and for life, since that love is always there. When you are in touch with that, life doesn't have to be any way other than the way it is. You don't need life to be special, because you feel good inside regardless of what's happening in the here and now.

Another thing the ego has difficulty accepting about reality is how little control it has over what is happening. The ego's defense is to pretend that it has more control than it actually does or to believe that it *should* have more control. But those lies don't hold up very well against reality, and believing those lies are one reason people suffer unnecessarily. Pretending and lying to yourself isn't a very good strategy for dealing with life.

If people simply accepted that they have little control—if they accepted reality—they wouldn't suffer over having so little control. Believing you should have control or that you need to be in control are the lies that make having little control so painful.

Having so little control isn't actually painful or a problem because something else much wiser and more loving than the ego is in control, and it's bringing you what you need to survive, thrive, grow, and evolve. It's the "grow and evolve" that can be difficult at times. But growing and evolving is like medicine: It's good for you even though it doesn't always go down easily.

In the end, life's challenges make you a better person, or they have the potential to do so. Remember, this is duality, which means that anything that's experienced as negative can also be experienced as positive. No experience is completely negative or completely positive. Every experience is "a mixed bag," so to speak.

The challenge is to find a way to perceive life positively rather than negatively. The ego sees the negative, while the divine self sees the positive. Both perspectives are valid, but one is more all-inclusive and pleasant. The positive perspective includes the negative, while the negative perspective overlooks the positive.

One of the lessons within duality is to learn to see the silver lining rather than just the cloud, to find the positive and then focus on that rather than the negative. Doing this, shifts you from the ego's perspective to the divine self's. In truth, in Oneness, there is only love. The negative is what you experience when you lose touch with love, when you lose touch with the truth, which is what happens in duality.

To be free of suffering, you don't have to transcend your negative thoughts and feelings altogether; you simply have to include a bigger, more positive perspective along with the negative. Include the positive with the negative so that you are seeing the whole picture and not just the ego's limited, negative perspective. When you are also aware of your divine self's perspective along with your ego's perspective, you won't suffer. It's seeing solely through the ego's eyes that leads to suffering.

The ego also has difficulty accepting change. As much as it would like to have a better and, therefore, different life and more and better of everything, the ego resists change at every turn. It doesn't want aging, death, or illness to be part of life (which is the body changing); it doesn't want others to change, unless they change in ways the ego likes; it doesn't want things to get old or break; and it doesn't like its routines disturbed.

When any of these things happens, the ego feels betrayed by life: "This shouldn't be happening!" it declares. But this is how life is. This is the life you get to have, the life you are being given: Life this way, not some other way. In duality, there is no ideal earth, no ideal life, and no ideal you.

The ego also suffers over wanting to change things that can't be changed, like how you look or your personality. Yes, you can modify things about your looks and your personality, but not fundamentally. How you look is how you look, and you can only do so much about that, no matter how much you wish it were otherwise.

The ego refuses to accept what *is* and often resists this by pretending that things *could* be different than they are, when they can't be. Or it plays the victim or is angry at life: "Poor me!" This is irrational and also causes a great deal of suffering.

What if, instead, you knew in your Heart that you are exactly as you are meant to be, and as such, you are perfect. That's the truth. You are as you are meant to be, and so is everyone and everything else.

Duality is duality—it has all kinds of different experiences, some that you like and some you don't like. Duality is like a playground that way: You get to have fun on the swings and you get to challenge yourself on the monkey bars, where you might fall. All of it is fun. You have to learn to find the fun in all of it: the fun in solving problems, overcoming difficulties, and finding new ways to see and do things.

So, what can you do about all this liking and not liking that the ego experiences? The trick is to see it from the divine self's perspective: You accept it and let it be as it is. You accept that the ego is constantly liking and not liking something. That's just what it does. The ego sees the world through a lens of what "I" like and what "I" don't like, which is what you hear the voice in your head saying so much of the time. You just need to remember that this "I" isn't you but your ego, your conditioning.

What if you always saw it this way? What if every time the voice in your head said "I," you knew it was your ego, not you? You would suffer very little. Let the voice in your head jabber away. Accept it. It's not you. You don't have to get rid of the voice in your head; you only have to realize that it isn't who you are. It's your programming, your ego. What a relief—because you can't get rid of that voice. But it will quiet down and become less unhappy and more positive over time the more you disengage from it.

Awareness of the programming is half the battle. But it isn't enough to see this voice as apart from you if you still respect it and see it as a voice of reason. You will still be stuck in the illusory world of the ego, listening to it. You have to see that this voice is not the voice of wisdom or truth but the opposite. You have to see that you can't trust it and you don't need it. Once you have clearly seen this, you will be truly free. But you will have to examine this voice again and again to discover the truth about it as fully as you need to.

The illusion is made up of ideas about how the ego *wants* things to be and how it thinks life *should* be rather than how they are. It holds up ideals and fantasies that life will never and can never live up to—because life is duality—and then it suffers over that fact. The illusion is made up of ideas of a perfect you, a perfect life, a perfect spouse, the perfect job, the perfect house, and so on. Everyone has their ideas about how they want their life to be, which life will never live up to—because nothing in life is perfect.

And so, people suffer. Without those ideas, there would be little suffering. The distance between your ideas about how life should be and how life actually is, is the degree to which you suffer. Once you see that these ideas—not life itself—are the cause of your suffering, you can begin to enjoy life just as it is. This is surrender: You surrender to the truth about life, the truth about reality, and then and only then will you find peace and happiness.

The ego also doesn't accept the fact—the reality—that it doesn't get to know things it wants to know. It especially wants to know what will happen in the future. "If only I knew that!" it wishes, as if that would make a difference! Often, the ego's desire to know the future is just an attempt to quell its fears or gain some sense of control.

But you aren't meant to know the future! Why? Because that would spoil the fun. Just like knowing how a movie or novel turns out, life is much more fun when you are unsure of what comes next. That's what's exciting about movies and novels, right?—that tension and excitement around what's going to happen next. That tension is fun!

You actually *love* not knowing, and you can experience the divine self loving this by simply tuning in to the subtle realm. It's just that the complaints of the voice in your head are much louder and more noticeable. But you can learn, instead, to turn your attention to the divine self's experience of life, which is one of joy.

The divine self loves this messy, unknowable life you are living. It loves not knowing for sure what you might choose or what someone else might choose. Who knows? Free will makes life unpredictable and interesting. Thank heavens for that. Imagine if life were predictable. What would be the point?

There's one other point I'd like to make before closing this chapter: You have been given the awareness and intelligence to see through the illusion and become free from it. This is the good news. In reality, life is really good! Once you are free of the illusion, you are free of suffering, since it was living in resistance to reality and denying the truth about reality that made life unpleasant. This is amazing, isn't it?!

You always could have been happy, but you had to discover the cause of your unhappiness. You thought you were unhappy because of the way things are, but instead, you see that your unhappiness was caused by your thoughts about the way things are.

The illusion is difficult to see through, but there is a way out, and each of you knows the way in your Heart. This is a beautiful life!

Conclusion

I know you are a sincere seeker. I have nothing but love for you. God has nothing but love for you. You are cherished by all of creation. *And* you are not human. We are the same. How can anything but love flow between us?

I and others like myself on higher dimensions are here for you. We never leave your side. We watch over you, protect you, heal you, guide you, and love you. You are our treasure, our Beloved. This love is your love too. It is in you just as it is in us, and nothing you can do can permanently obscure it or separate you from it.

In our eyes, you are perfect just as you are. There is nothing you have to change; and yet, change is happening everywhere in the universe, and it cannot be otherwise. We are on a glorious journey together toward expansion and greater love and more of everything that is good.

Everything in duality is evolving toward greater love and goodness and leaving pain and suffering behind. Those of us in Oneness are evolving too. By sharing in this way with you, we are able to manifest the love that we are and grow in greater wisdom and compassion.

There is no end to love, to wisdom, or to compassion. There is no end to life. It is eternal. You are eternal. Please remember this in your darker moments, when the light in you dims and you feel small and separate. Please remember how we care for you and how deeply we love you. Remember that you are light, and look for that light within you, no matter how tiny a spark it might be. Focus on it, and it will grow. Like an ember you gently bring to life with your breath, your attention will reignite your light and bring you back to love and peace.

You are never lost, no matter how lost you may feel, for we are right here by your side. You are never alone, and there is nothing to fear. Relax, be at peace now, and know your greatness, your divinity, as we do.

AFTERWORD

About the Channeled Books by Jesus

Many are curious about how my channeled books by Jesus are written, so I'll say a little about that. I receive the books from Jesus in the same way that Helen Schucman received *A Course in Miracles*, which is also said to be dictated by Jesus. Many others have also received their writings this way, including St. Teresa of Avila, St. Hildegard de Bingen, Richard Bach, and Neale Donald Walsch. This method of receiving information is called conscious channeling. It's a process of hearing words mentally and writing them down as they are heard, without any thought. I can receive this communication anywhere. I don't need to be in a meditative or trance state. All that's necessary is that I don't think.

When I'm receiving this dictation, it's as if Jesus is sitting in a chair next to me speaking the words, except that those words are heard mentally. I can ask questions during this dictation and receive answers, but the process works best when my own mind is completely set aside. Then the flow happens smoothly and rapidly and without interruption until a particular stopping place is reached.

When I'm writing a book, I usually write 700-1500 words each morning and then go over that later the same day, adding necessary punctuation and paragraphing. The words require very little editing, nor do I change anything in the organization of the book. The books are given to me without me knowing what the book will include, although I'm given a table of contents.

Writing this way is a little like driving blind, in that I don't know what's coming next, although I might have an intuitive sense of it. It takes continual trust that the book will come together, which it always does. I couldn't have written these books by myself. My books are my teachers, and I am privileged to share them.

Many also wonder how I came to be a channel for Jesus, so I'll share a little about that too. I didn't ask for or necessarily desire to be a channel for Jesus, and I had no idea my work would take this turn. Life is full of surprises! However, in 2012, a spiritual shift and deepening happened, and I became aware of a profound connection to the Christian lineage that went back many lifetimes for me. That year, in the fall, Mother Mary appeared to me. I saw her and spoke with her. She said she would like me to write a small book for her and that Jesus would also be in contact soon.

Subsequently, I began having inner experiences of Mother Mary, Jesus, and a circle of twenty-six other Ascended Masters, who appeared to me in my mind's eye and spoke to me in words I could clearly hear in my mind. The reason they gave me for appearing at that time is that I had reached a point in my growth and in my life when I would be working more closely with them. Here are a few of the inner experiences I had in 2013 with Mother Mary and Jesus, which I recorded in my spiritual log:

"Jesus's face materialized, just for a few seconds, and he began to talk with me. I saw this in my mind's eye and I heard his words inside my head. Jesus said that he and various Ascended Masters were behind my work and that I'd prepared for this role as a channel for eons. He said they are healing the world through the words I and others write and that words are especially powerful today because they can reach so many people. When Jesus spoke, I could feel how huge he is as a spiritual being. He is one of the main guardians of this planet. He has explained to me that he is available to all who are devoted to him and to anyone who calls upon him."

On another occasion, I recorded this:

"I felt and saw in my mind's eye a circle of beings around me who were Ascended Masters. They looked like a circle of light beings. Although they were indistinct figures, a sense of sacredness and holiness permeated the gathering. They were conveying intuitively to me a sense of celebration, like a birthday. There was a flame above each of their heads and above mine, as I stood in the center of the circle. The scene looked a little like a birthday cake, and I wondered if the candles on birthday cakes symbolized a new birth or new phase, as this seemed to. I was told that it was an initiation. After a few moments, they began to leave, one by one, and only one remained. It was Jesus. He said, 'Welcome, my beloved child,' and held out his arms. 'You are part of this circle now. You have arrived at your destination. We will always be with you. You will receive training soon.'"

It was later explained to me that the training Jesus was speaking about was in being an instrument of his teachings and a transmitter for Christ Consciousness, and that this training would happen while I was asleep and at other times.

And on another day, this is what I wrote:

"In my meditation, I felt moved to call on Mother Mary. She appeared to me and said: 'Blessed One, I have a blessing for you and a rose.' I then saw, in my mind's eye, her hand me a red rose. 'The rose is a symbol of love and connection with all and with me. When you see a rose, think of me,' she said. The blessing she gave me felt like molasses moving slowly down my body from head to toe."

Later, I learned from a religious scholar that the rose in Christianity is like the lotus in Hinduism and that Mary is often seen with roses. Roses were part of the miracle performed by the Virgin of Guadalupe, and Mother Mary is often depicted with roses at her feet. Furthermore, a rose is often depicted at the center of the cross. On another occasion, Mary placed a wreath of roses on my head and called me her child and said she would be there to greet and embrace me at the end of my life. It felt very heavenly and like I had always known her.

There is a purity in the experience of these beings and in their communication. They are loving, accepting, and very respectful of our free will. I see them inwardly, feel them, and hear them with distinct voices and energies. I've been channeling since 1986, so I have experience with the various beings in other dimensions, including the false ones, which I talked about in my batgap.com interview, which you can listen to on my website.

When I first started working with Jesus, I asked him if I should acknowledge him as the author, being somewhat concerned about what people might think about claiming this. He said I was free to choose not to do these books, but if I chose to, he wanted people to know that these were his words. He wanted people to have a direct and personal experience of him.

I see now that having these books be in his voice has made them more powerful than if they had been in my voice.

I was also concerned about the negative associations many "spiritual but not religious" people might have around Jesus and Christianity because of Christianity's emphasis on fear, guilt, and judgment. But it is these very distortions of the teachings of Jesus and the wounds they've caused that Jesus now wishes to correct and heal through the books we are writing together.

Another question I'm often asked is: "How do you know it's Jesus?" Lower astral entities simply could not nor would they write a book like the ones I'm bringing through, although they could regurgitate a few phrases of perennial wisdom they gathered along the way if that would facilitate their con. Writing a book wouldn't be fun for them, and it's too lengthy a project. But more importantly, they aren't wise enough to do this. So, when an entire book comes through that is consistently wise and said to be from Jesus, then it is Jesus, because those capable of such wisdom wouldn't misrepresent themselves: "By their fruits, you will know them."

However, it is still possible for even developed channels to make mistakes, so your discrimination is important. But that doesn't mean you have to "throw the baby out with the bathwater" if something doesn't ring true. Ultimately, you must decide for yourself what you will believe. That is one of our lessons as human beings.

Another reason I know I am speaking to Jesus, besides the fact that he identifies himself as Jesus, is that beings on other dimensions have a unique energy signature, and when you are a developed channel, you can recognize the signature of who you are talking with.

There are other ways you can tell the level of the being you are talking with. For instance, higher beings never tell you what to do, while lower astral beings do exactly that. Lower beings flatter you while disempowering you and suggesting that you do things that will harm yourself. Higher beings support you, advise you wisely, and have your best interests at heart.

Undeveloped channels or channels who are ego-identified or in a negative state need to be aware of the dangers of channeling. The danger is that they will reach only astral beings, who are con artists and worse. Lower astral beings will claim to be Jesus and other Ascended Masters and then deliver inaccurate information and information that Jesus and other Ascended Masters would not. You can recognize lower astral beings because they create fear, confusion, and a sense of victimhood in those they are speaking to. The best preparation for being a channel is meditation and a sincere devotion to God and a lack of ego-identification. Be wary of channels who are not devoted in these ways.

Jesus is available to everyone who is devoted to him and his message of love. He is in touch with many, many people, although not as many can actually speak with him. He is speaking through a number of channels today because his message is so needed. He is very involved with the transformation of consciousness on this planet, along with many other Ascended Masters.

Any differences in the many books written that are said to be from Jesus are likely due to differences in the channels' backgrounds and vocabularies. Channels are instruments, and those instruments affect what comes through and how clearly it comes through. A channel's interests, audience, and openness to certain kinds of information are other factors that affect what information comes through or doesn't come through.

I happily and gratefully share these words from Jesus and my relationship with him with you because it has so enriched me, and I can only hope that it will do the same for you. So, there you have it!

About the Author

Gina Lake is a nondual spiritual teacher and the author of over twenty books about awakening to one's true nature. She is also a gifted intuitive and channel with a master's degree in Counseling Psychology and over twenty-five years' experience supporting people in their spiritual growth. In 2012, Jesus began dictating books through her. These teachings from Jesus are based on universal truth, not on any religion. Her website offers information about her books and online courses, a free ebook, and audio and video recordings:

www.RadicalHappiness.com

Christ Consciousness Transmission (CCT) Online Weekly Meetings

Transmission is something that naturally happens from spiritual teacher to aspirant and from beings on higher dimensions to those who are willing to receive on this dimension. Transmission has been used throughout the ages to accelerate spiritual evolution and raise consciousness. In the process, emotional and sometimes physical healing also take place, as a clearing of energy blocks from the energy field is a necessary and natural part of raising consciousness.

In weekly online Zoom video meetings, Gina Lake and her husband offer Christ Consciousness transmissions. This is one of the ways that Jesus and the other Ascended Masters working with Jesus intend to raise humanity's level of consciousness. A channeled message from Jesus is given before the transmission to prepare, teach, and inspire those who are there to receive the transmission. Many report feeling a transmission come through these channeled messages as well.

The transmission takes around twenty minutes and is done in silence except for some music, which is meant to help people open and receive. During the transmission, Gina Lake and her husband are simply acting as antennas for Christ Consciousness, as it streams to earth to be received by all who are willing to open to and be uplifted by divine grace. Since there is actually no such thing as time and space, these are not a barrier to receiving the transmission, which works as well online as in person. You can find out more about these transmissions on Gina's website at:

www.RadicalHappiness.com/transmissions

If you enjoyed this book, we think you will also enjoy these other books from Jesus by Gina Lake...

The Jesus Trilogy. In this trilogy by Jesus, are three jewels, each shining in its own way and illuminating the same truth: You are not only human but divine, and you are meant to flourish and love one another. In words that are for today, Jesus speaks intimately and directly to the reader of the secrets to peace, love, and happiness. He explains the deepest of all mysteries: who you are and how you can live as he taught long ago. The three books in The Jesus Trilogy were dictated to Gina Lake by Jesus and include *Choice and Will, Love and Surrender,* and *Beliefs, Emotions, and the Creation of Reality*. The books in the trilogy are also available individually and can be read in any order.

In the World but Not of It: New Teachings from Jesus on Embodying the Divine: From the Introduction, by Jesus: "What I have come to teach now is that you can embody love, as I did. You can become Christ within this human life and learn to embody all that is good within you. I came to show you the beauty of your own soul and what is possible as a human. I came to show you that it is possible to be both human and divine, to be love incarnate. You are equally both. You walk with one foot in the world of form and another in the Formless. This mysterious duality within your being is what this book is about." This book is another in a series of books dictated to Gina Lake by Jesus.

For more information about Gina's books, please visit:
www.RadicalHappiness.com/books

Awakening Now Online Course

It's time to start living what you've been reading about. Are you interested in delving more deeply into the teachings in Gina Lake's books, receiving ongoing support for waking up, and experiencing the power of Christ Consciousness transmissions? You'll find that and much more in the Awakening Now online course:

This course was created for your awakening. The methods presented are powerful companions on the path to enlightenment and true happiness. Awakening Now will help you experience life through fresh eyes and discover the delight of truly being alive. This 100-day inner workout is packed with both time-honored and original practices that will pull the rug out from under your ego and wake you up. You'll immerse yourself in materials, practices, guided meditations, and inquiries that will transform your consciousness. And in video webinars, you'll receive transmissions of Christ Consciousness. These transmissions are a direct current of love and healing that will accelerate your evolution and help you break through to a new level of being. By the end of 100 days, you will have developed new habits and ways of being that will result in being more richly alive and present and greater joy and equanimity.

www.RadicalHappiness.com/online-courses

More Books by Gina Lake

Available in paperback, ebook, and audiobook formats.

Jesus Speaking Series: In this series of four channeled audiobooks/books by Jesus, narrated by Gina Lake, Jesus speaks to us from another dimension to awaken Christ Consciousness within us. In this series, Jesus shows us how we can become more Christ-like and live as he did. These are nondual (Oneness) teachings and not based on any religion. Jesus explains:

> *"I am speaking to you now through this channel to help you to know of my presence and feel my presence in your life more fully. My intention is to help you realize your true nature and to live as the best human being you can be. Allow me to be your guide back home to love."*

A Heroic Life: New Teachings from Jesus on the Human Journey. The hero's journey—this human life—is a search for the greatest treasure of all: the gifts of your true nature. These gifts are your birthright, but they have been hidden from you, kept from you by the dragon: the ego. These gifts are the wisdom, love, peace, courage, strength, and joy that reside at your core. *A Heroic Life* shows you how to overcome the ego's false beliefs and face the ego's fears. It provides you with both a perspective and a map to help you successfully and happily navigate life's challenges and live heroically. This book is another in a series of books dictated to Gina Lake by Jesus.

All Grace: New Teachings from Jesus on the Truth About Life. Grace is the mysterious and unseen movement of God upon creation, which is motivated by love and indistinct from love. *All Grace* was given to Gina Lake by Jesus and represents his wisdom and understanding of life. It is about the magnificent and incomprehensible force behind life, which created life, sustains it, and operates within it as you and me and all of creation. *All Grace* is full of profound and life-changing truth.

From Stress to Stillness: Tools for Inner Peace. Most stress is created by how we think about things. *From Stress to Stillness* will help you to examine what you are thinking and change your relationship to your thoughts so that they no longer result in stress. Drawing from the wisdom traditions, psychology, New Thought, and the author's own experience as a spiritual teacher and counselor, *From Stress to Stillness* offers many practices and suggestions that will lead to greater peace and equanimity, even in a busy and stress-filled world.

Embracing the Now: Finding Peace and Happiness in What Is*.* The Now—this moment—is the true source of happiness and peace and the key to living a fulfilled and meaningful life. *Embracing the Now* is a collection of essays that can serve as daily reminders of the deepest truths. Full of clear insight and wisdom, *Embracing the Now* explains how the mind keeps us from being in the moment, how to move into the Now and stay there, and what living from the Now is like. It also explains how to overcome stumbling blocks to being in the Now, such as fears, doubts, misunderstandings, judgments, distrust of life, desires, and other conditioned ideas that are behind human suffering.

Radical Happiness: A Guide to Awakening provides the keys to experiencing the happiness that is ever-present and not dependent on circumstances. This happiness comes from realizing that who you think you are is not who you really are. *Radical Happiness* describes the nature of the egoic state of consciousness and how it interferes with happiness, what awakening and enlightenment are, and how to live in the world after awakening.

Living in the Now: How to Live as the Spiritual Being That You Are. The 99 essays in *Living in the Now* will help you realize your true nature and live as that. They answer many questions raised by the spiritual search and offer wisdom on subjects such as fear, anger, happiness, aging, boredom, desire, patience, forgiveness, acceptance, love, commitment, meditation, being present, emotions, trusting your Heart, and many other deep subjects. These essays will help you become more conscious, present, happy, loving, grateful, at peace, and fulfilled.

Return to Essence: How to Be in the Flow and Fulfill Your Life's Purpose describes how to get into the flow and stay there and how to live life from there. Being in the flow and not being in the flow are two very different states. One is dominated by the ego-driven mind, which is the cause of suffering, while the other is the domain of Essence, the Divine within each of us. You are meant to live in the flow. The flow is the experience of Essence—your true self—as it lives life through you and fulfills its purpose for this life.

Being Happy (Even When You Don't Get What You Want): The Truth About Manifesting and Desires will help you discriminate between your Heart's desires and the ego's and relate to the ego's desires in a way that reduces suffering and increases joy. By pointing out the myths about desire that keep us tied to our ego's desires and the suffering they cause, *Being Happy (Even When You Don't Get What You Want)* will help you be happy regardless of your desires and whether you are attaining them. So *Being Happy* is also about spiritual freedom, or liberation, which comes from following the Heart, our deepest desires, instead of the ego's desires. It is about becoming a lover of life rather than a desirer.

Getting Free: Moving Beyond Negativity and Limiting Beliefs. To a large extent, healing our conditioning involves changing our relationship to our mind and discovering who we really are. *Getting Free* will help you do that. It will also help you reprogram your mind; clear negative thoughts and self-images; use meditation, prayer, forgiveness, and gratitude; work with spiritual forces to assist healing and clear negativity; and heal entrenched issues from the past.

Choosing Love: Moving from Ego to Essence in Relationships. Having a truly meaningful relationship requires choosing love over your conditioning: your ideas, fantasies, desires, images, and beliefs. *Choosing Love* describes how to move beyond judgment, anger, romantic illusions, and differences to love and oneness with another. It explains how to drop into your Being, where Oneness and love exist, and be with others from there.

For more information, please visit the "Books" page at

www.RadicalHappiness.com

Made in the USA
Coppell, TX
22 September 2020